A CLASSIC CHINESE READER

MASTERS ON THE RECORDS OF THE GRAND HISTORIAN

COMPILED
BY EDITORIAL BOARD
OF CHINESE LITERATURE AND HISTORY

TRANSLATED BY WANG LI AND LI LI

CHINA INTERCONTINENTAL PRESS   ZHONGHUA BOOK COMPANY

Sima Qian and the *Records of the Grand Historian*

An Pingqiu

The basin of the Yellow River, which historically traces back to the ancient times, is the cradle of many Chinese talents. Sima Qian was one of them. He was the great historian, litterateur and ideologist who lived in the period under the reign of Emperor Wu of Han Dynasty (more than 2,000 years ago). He was born in Longmen, located near the middle of the Yellow River.

Longmen is a poetic and mysterious place. The Yellow

River resembles a roaring yellow dragon running from north to south. There is the Longmen Mountain on the left bank and the Liangshan Mountain on the right bank, like two gates beside the rushing water. It was said that only the holy dragon could jump over the "gates". That's why the place was named Longmen (meaning the dragon gates). According to legends, the "dragon gates" were made under the order of Yu for controlling the flood and clearing the Yellow River. Therefore, it is also called the "Yu Gate". Sima Qian spent his childhood in the south of Xiayang City, Zuopingyi, southwest of Longmen (current Zhichuan Town, Hancheng County, Shaanxi), doing farm work and herding cattle. He loved reading and studying. In the first year of the Jianyuan period under the reign of Emperor Wu of Han Dynasty (140 B.C.), six-year-old Sima Qian went to Chang'an (the capital city) together with his father Sima Tan. At that time, the Western Han Dynasty had entered a period of great prosperity.

Many remote ancestors of Sima Tan served as official historians. From 140 B.C. to 110 B.C., Sima Tan served as the *Taishiling* (title of official historian), who was in charge of compiling the national history. Sima Tan received vast amounts of education, covering astronomy, calendar, laws and regulations and literary quotations. He was the author of the significant academic work titled *On the Principal Ideas Comprised within the Six Schools* (*Lun Liu Jia Yao Zhi*), providing insightful comments on the major academic schools in pre-Qin period. Sima Tan decided to write a historical book, because there had been no compilation of national history for many years and stories of numerous outstanding people had not been recorded. He made full preparation starting with the conception to the collection of historical materials, and wrote several chapters. It should be said that the *Records of the Grand Historian* of Sima Qian was based on the work of Sima Tan.

Sima Qian received his education directly by his father. He had read many books even when he was only ten years old. Then, he began to study ancient Chinese proses and literatures, including *The Book of Documents (Shang Shu), The Commentary of Zuo (Zuo Zhuan), The Discourses of the States (Guo Yu)*and *The Origin of the World (Shi Ben)*. He studied hard and became knowledgeable. Great aspiration and patriotism to his country lead him to launch a nationwide trip for a field survey at the age of 20.

Leaving Chang'an, Sima Qian visited the Miluo River to worship the patriotic Chinese poet Qu Yuan, who committed suicide by drowning himself in the river. Then, he climbed up the Jiuyi Mountain to visit the tomb of Shun, a legendary monarch in ancient China. Later, he visited Mount Lushan in the south for a survey on the history of the dredging projects carried out at Jiujiang under the order of Yu. To the southeast, he visited the

Kuaiji Mountain, where Yu had a meeting with the dukes and held the investiture for the contributors. He even visited the Yu Cave. At the Wu area, he visited the old residence of Huang Xie, the Lord of Chunshen, who was one of the four well-known princes in the Warring States period. He said, "The palace was so grand!" In addition, Sima Qian also visited Huaiyin (the hometown of Han Xin), the Huai River and the Sishui River, and Qufu (the capital of the Lu State), where he saw the Temple of Confucius and showed great respect and admiration to the local atmosphere highlighting education and rites. He passed through the areas waged with frequent wars, such as those between the Qi, Lu, Liang and Chu states (currently Shandong, northern Jiangsu and eastern Henan). Finally, he traveled westward to ruins of Daliang (currently northwest of Kaifeng, Henan province), the capital of the Wei State, and visited the Yi Gate, where the Lord of Xinling drove a carriage to invite Hou Ying. He said, "No wonder the Lord of Xinling is so well-known. He deserves the reputation."After that, he returned to Chang'an.

Soon after his return to Chang'an, Sima Qian was appointed *Langzhong* (one of the companion officials of the emperor). Although it was not a high-ranking position, there was more chance for him to accompany Emperor Wu of Han Dynasty to visit many places, including the Kongtong Mountain in the west (currently west of

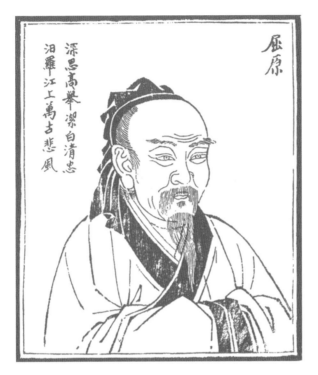

Portrait of Qu Yuan

Pingliang County, Gansu), Mount Taishan in the east, Jieshi at the seaside, and Jiuyuan (current the area near Wuyuan County of Inner Mongolia) beyond the Great Wall in the north. In the sixth year of the Yuanding period under the reign of Emperor Wu of Han Dynasty (111 B.C.), under the orders of the court, Sima Qian visited the south of the Ba and Shu areas, and then even farther to Kunming. This enabled him to have a good understanding of the social conditions in the southwestern area. Through these trips, Sima Qian expanded his horizon and got the chance to communicate directly with people and visited many historical sites to collect historical materials, which later became a solid foundation for the *Records of the Grand Historian*.

Sima Qian got back from the southwestern area in the first year of the Yuanfeng period under the reign of Emperor Wu of Han Dynasty (110 B.C.). He soon arrived at Zhounan (currently the area near Luoyang) between the Yellow River and the Luoshui River to meet his father, who was laying in his deathbed. Sima Tan held his son's hand and cried. He asked him to finish the book that he could not finish and bear the task to write the historical records. Shortly after, Sima Tan died.

Three years later (108 B.C.), 38-year-old Sima Qian succeeded his father's position as the *Taishiling*. Taking the chance, he began taking out excerpts from the ancient historical records and classics from the national archives and libraries. At the same time, he visited people who were well versed in history, in order to make amendments and add supplement to historical facts. In the first year of the Taichu period under the reign of Emperor Wu of Han Dynasty (104 B.C.), Sima Qian took charge of the calendar reform and made the *Taichu Calendar*. At the age of 42, when his thoughts have matured, with great concentration he began to write the *Records of the Grand Historian*.

However, the tragedy began in the seventh year (the third year of the Tianhan period under the reign of

Emperor Wu of Han Dynasty, namely 98 B.C.) of writing historical records. In the second year of the Tianhan Period, Emperor Wu of Han Dynasty sent Ershi General Li Guangli to fight against the Huns. Li Guangli ordered Li Ling, who was the then-commandant-in-chief of the cavalry, to lead 5,000 infantry members to enter the enemy territory. The troop was outnumbered and defeated after fighting against the Huns for more than ten days. Without weapons and assistance, the soldiers surrendered. After receiving the news, some officials began to slander Li Ling. However, Sima Qian believed that the slander towards Li Ling was undeserved as Li Ling had fought hard against the enemy and surrendered, only because there were no other alternatives. He also believed that Li Ling would find a proper chance to serve the Han Dynasty again.Sima Qian voiced his opinion to Emperor Wu. Emperor Wu burst into anger, because he believed that Sima Qian was deliberately defaming Li Guangli, who was the brother of the imperial concubine Mrs Li, and absolving Li Ling from the guilt of surrender. Sima Qian was imprisoned subsequently. The year after he was castrated and imprisoned in a dark room. It was a great insult to Sima Qian, who wrote his grief and indignation in the letter to his friend Ren An. He said, "I suffered this misfortune because of what I had said, and then become the laughingstock of people in my hometown. I desecrated the ancestors. I am so ashamed that I dare not to visit my parents' tombs again. Even after hundred years I will just be more ashamed. Every time I think about it, my back is full of sweat, soaking my clothes." However, in order to continue his writing, he was not depressed by such suffering. He knew that many sages in the history suffered difficulties but were determined to fulfill their aspiration. Afterwards, he was relieved from the distress and he continued to write the great book. He was appointed *Zhongshuling* (official title) upon his release from prison. He thought, "The book will compensate my early sufferings. As long as it is finished, it would not matter even if I were killed a thousand times. I will never regret it." He worked even harder to finish the book. In the fourth year of the Taishi period under the reign of Emperor Wu of Han Dynasty (93 B.C.), the 53-year-old Sima Qian finished the first historical book that was ever to be written. Unfortunately, soon after that, the great historian died. The work was made public by his grandson Yang Yun during the reign of Emperor Xuan of Han Dynasty.

The *Records of the Grand Historian* was first named *Tai Shi Gong Shu* and *Tai Shi Gong Ji*. It was China's first general historical work presented in series of biographies. The historical works before were written in chronological order, such as *The Spring and Autumn Annals* (*Chun Qiu*), or history of individual countries, such as *The Discourses of the States* and *The Strategies of the Warring States* (*Zhan Guo Ce*). However, the *Records of the Grand*

Historian centers around people, including biographies of emperors (called *Benji*) and biographies of common people (called *Liezhuan*). The later historical works, from *The History of the Han Dynasty* (Han Shu) *to The Draft History of Qing* (*Qing Shi Gao*), followed suit such style. The *Records of the Grand Historian* is not a dynastic historical work. Instead, it is a general historical work covering 3,000 years from the period under the reign of Yellow Emperor to the Taichu period under the reign of Emperor Wu of Han Dynasty. It consists of 12 *Benji* (royal annals), 10 *Biao* (historical tables), eight *Shu* (monographs), 30 *Shijia* (genealogies of noble houses) and 70 *Liezhuan* (biographies), 130 chapters in all, with 526,500 Chinese characters. Ban Gu wrote in *The History of the Han Dynasty: the Biography of Sima Qian* that ten chapters of the *Records of the Grand Historian* were lost. The *Records of the Grand Historian* today consists of 130 chapters, with the lost chapters supplemented by Chu Shaosun and other scholars who lived in the period under the reign of Emperor Yuan and Emperor Cheng of Han Dynasty.

The "royal annals" includes a chronicle of events to show achievements, words and actions of the emperors of different dynasties, starting from the period of the Five Emperors (the Yellow Emperor, Zhuanxu, Ku, Yao and Shun) to the period under the reign of Emperor Wu of Han Dynasty. The "historical tables" are records of

9

Ancient Chinese star map

the people and historical events in the form of tables, supplementing the royal annals and the biographical accounts. The "historical tables" can be classified into chronological tables, genealogical tables and monthly tables. The chronological tables were compiled by time, such as *The Annual Table of the Six Feudal States* (*Liu Guo Nian Biao*) and *The Annual Form of the Famous Ministers and Generals Since Han Dynasty* (*Han Xing Yi Lai Jiang Xiang Ming Chen Nian Biao*). The genealogical tables were compiled due to the difficulties recording age-old people and events by time, such as the *Genealogical Table of the Three Ages* (*San Dai Shi Biao*). The monthly table refers to the *Monthly Table of the Events between Qin and Chu* (*Qin Chu Zhi Ji Yue Biao*), which was made because of the ever-changing events during the struggling times between Chu and Han, for which records by time could not reflect the richness of the history. The"monographs" are treatises on particular subjects. For example, *As tronomy* (*Tian Guan Shu*) is about astronomy and As tronomy, while the *Rivers and Canals* (*He Qu Shu*) is about water systems and water conservancy projects. The "genealogies of noble houses" are records of the history of princedoms, such as the *House of King Goujian of Yue* (*Yue Wang Goujian Shi Jia*) and the *House of Marquis of Liu* (*Liu Hou Shi Jia*). The "biographies" mainly consist of biographies of important people. There are: special biographies, each of them about one person, such as the *Biography of the Marquis of Huaiyin* (*Huaiyin Hou Liezhuan*); combined biographies, each of which is about two or more people, such as the *Biographies of Lian Po and Lin Xiangru* (*Lian Po Lin XiangRu Liezhuan*); biographies of people belonging to the same type, regardless of whether they lived in the same period, such as the *Biographies of Knight-errants* (*You Xia Liezhuan*); affiliated biographies. In addition, there are also some treatises describing the Chinese ethnic groups and the neighboring countries, and regions that communicated with the Han Dynasty, such as the *Treatise on the Eastern Yue* (*Dong Yue Liezhuan*) and the *Treatise on the Xiongnu* (*Xiongnu Liezhuan*). The five parts mentioned above, namely the royal annals, historical tables, monographs, genealogies of noble houses and biographies, form the complete system of the *Records of the Grand Historian*. The author not only indicated his own viewpoints in the narrations, but also commented on the history with simplicity at the end of each chapter (See "The Grand Historian's Remarks").

The author not only aimed to record the historical events and people, but wanted to explore the relationship between nature, and the human affairs as well as the historical evolution. The book reflects the knowledge and experience of the historian who lived 2,000 years ago. Due to lack of 'correct' theoretical guidance, it was difficult for him to make the right conclusion.As a historical book, the *Records of the Grand Historian* is praiseworthy, because the author had done a thorough job on the historical materials, and has been faithful to the facts. Sima Qian made a careful analysis and reviewed huge amounts of written materials to eliminate the false and retain the true. He never judged a person by his success or failure and never go with the stream. He did not sing groundless praises of anyone or conceal any evildoers and bad deeds,shortcomings or mistakes. He paid great respect to Confucius. However, he criticized Confucius for his preposterous and groundless praises of contemporary historical figures and events in *The Spring and Autumn Annals*. There is another example. Concerning Liu Bang, the first emperor of the Western Han Dynasty, he revealed the emperor's foresight, generosity, open-mindedness and talent in discovering capable people, and putting them at suitable posts. However, he also vividly described the emperor to be mischievous. That is why the *Records of the Grand Historian* is recognized as a faithful historical account through the ages.

The book reflects the author's progressive thought and clear cut stand on what to love and what to hate. When writing about Lin Xiangru,who returned the jade intact to the State of Zhao, Sima Qian depicted a figure that safeguarded the dignity of his country with his wisdom and courage. He praised Lin Xiangru for his nobility to put the country's interest first.When writing about Li Guang, who was a patriotic general, he highly praised him. The historian displayed his sorrow and sympathy towards the general when the general was marginalized by the court and ultimately committed suicide to avoid suffering from dishonor. Sima Qian gave full affirmation to the knight-errants, who lived among the people and followed the principles of "standing by one's words and not stopping one's action until success is achieved; keeping promise and helping others even sacrificing their own lives" and "never showing off their own abilities and merits". On the other hand, he sharply ridiculed the cruel officials who made emperors' will as a binding law. He liked and respected the Lord of Xinling (named Wuji) of the Wei State very much so that he called him *"gongzi"*(a very respectful title for man) for 47 times in the *Biography of the Prince of Wei* for a sharp contrast between the Lord of Xinling and other contemporary bigwigs.

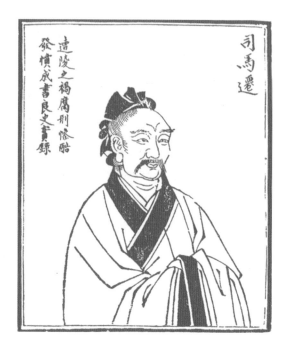

Sima Qian

When writing the *Records of the Grand Historian,* Sima Qian devised a way to present history in series of biographies. This was done by writing biographical literature by combining depiction of figures with description of scenes. He recorded the historical events in a faithful and vivid way, such as the "Fire Bull Strategy", "the Emperor and the Assassin", the "Banquet at Hongmen" and the "Battle of Gaixia", which are not only historical records but also recreated literature with specific scenes and vivid figures, and until this day it is universally praised. That's why Lu Xun said the *Records of the Grand Historian* is a masterpiece of historical works and on par with the *Lisao*

14

(one of the works by Qu Yuan) even without rhyme.

In history, many people made annotations for the *Records of the Grand Historian*. Of them, the most famous ones are Pei Yin (the Liu-Song Dynasty of the Southern Dynasties), who is the author of the *Collection of Annotations on the Records of the Grand Historian* (*Shiji Jijie*), Sima Zhen (Tang Dynasty), who is the author of the *Elucidation of the Records of the Grand Historian* (*Shiji Suoyin*), and Zhang Shoujie (Tang Dynasty), who is the author of the *Correct Interpretation of the Records of the Grand Historian* (*Shiji Zhengyi*). They made separate annotations, which were attached to text of the *Records of the Grand Historian* in the Northern Song Dynasty. The version of the *Records of the Grand Historian* with punctuations that we usually use today was edited by Zhonghua Book Company based on the *Block-Printed Edition of the Collection of Annotations, Elucidation and Correct Interpretation of the Records of the Grand Historian* (Shiji Jijie Suoyin Zhengyi Hekeben) published by Jinling Publishing House during the reign of Emperor Tongzhi of the Qing Dynasty.

The *Records of the Grand Historian* is a valuable cultural heritage of the Chinese nation and cherished by all the Chinese people and even globally. The spirit of Sima Qian and his work will be immortal and forever glorious.

Two ways to read the *Records of the Grand Historian*

Liang Qichao

The first way to read the *Records of the Grand Historian*

There are two ways to read the *Records of the Grand Historian*: reading for common knowledge and reading for specialized study. Both ways of reading can be started with the same preparation.

Read *The Preface of Shi Ji (Taishigong Zi Xu)* and The *History of the Han Dynasty: the Biography of Sima*

Qian (*Han Shu: Sima Qian Zhuan*) first to understand the period when the author lived, the personality, behaviors and experience of the author, and the overview of the book.

Then, read the part of The *History of the Han Dynasty:Autobiography (Han Shu: Xu Zhuan)* about the *Records of the Grand Historian*, the *Chapter on the Six Schools (Liu Jia Pian)*, the *Chapter on the Two Literary Forms (Er Ti Pian)* and the *Chapter on Official History (Zheng Shi Pian)* in the *Comments on Historical Records (Shi Tong)* by Liu Zhiji, the part of the *General Records: Foreword (Tong Zhi: Zong Xu)* by Zheng Qiao about the *Records of the Grand Historian*, the parts of official history in the *History of Sui Dynasty: the Confucian Classics (Sui Shu: Jing Ji Zhi)* and the *Bibliography of the Complete Library in the Four Branches of Literature (Si Ku Ti Yao)* about the *Records of the Grand Historian* to have a brief understanding of the significance and value of the book in the historian circle.

Here we start with reading for common knowledge.

The *Records of the Grand Historian* set an example for the following historical records. It is the first well-organized ancient historical book with clear tenet. The language is so beautiful. For 2,000 years, it has been so embraced by the scholars that it has become one of the books for the people to acquire common knowledge, with significance comparable with the six Confucian classics.

Therefore, every student read it. However, it is so long and complicated to read. To save efforts and time, I excerpted the following parts for reading first:

For the 10 tables, only read the forewords, without in-depth study of the content. Pay attention to the style and compare the tables with each other to find the similarity and difference in the ways of compilation and preparation.

The eight monographs composed an extremely important part of the book. However, the versions today seem not to be the originals. So, it is better to read the records in The *History of the Han Dynasty* than reading them, which can be completely ignored.

The chapters about the Wu, Qi, Lu, Guan Cai, Chen Qi, Wei, Song, Jin, Chu, Yue and Zheng among the genealogies of noble houses were nearly completely sourced from *The Commentary of Zuo*. So, people who have read *The Commentary of Zuo* need not to read these chapters. However, the genealogies about the noble houses of the Warring States must be read, because there is no systematic mention of them in the *Strategies of the Warring States*.

The *Annals of the Five Emperors (Wu Di Ji)*, the *Biographies of Soothsayers (Ri Zhe Zhuan)* and the *Biographies of Diviners (Gui Ce Zhuan)* have been proved to be pseudo graphs, which are disordered, plain and vulgar. So, it is not necessary to read them. Some long chapters, like the *Biographies of Bian Que and Duke (Tai)*

Portrait of Liang Qichao

Cang (*Bian Que Cang Gong Zhuan*), seem not to be the final editions. So, it is enough to get a brief understanding of them.

The part selected based on the abovementioned principles accounts about one third of the book. In this way, it saves a lot of efforts to read. The rest part can be read in the way as follows.

The first is to read it for purpose of study on editorial form and tenet. The *Records of the Grand Historian* consists of a mixing of the genres in extremely complicated forms, boasting wide coverage. For example, the "biographies" cover nearly all the aspects of the social culture, including the representative political figures as well as the people in the academic and art circles. Compared with the *Seven Abstracts* (*Qi Lüe*) collated by Liu Xiang, the *Biographies of the Disciples of Zhongni*

(*Zhongni Di Zi Zhuan*) and the Biographies of Lao-Tzu, Chuang-Tzu, Shen-Tze (Shen Buhai) and Hanfeizi (Lao Zhuang Shen Han Zhuan) are more specific than the works of the academic schools in the pre-Qin period; the *Biographies of Confucian Scholars (Ru Lin Lie Zhuan)* is more detailed than the original narrations of the academic schools in the Qin and Han Dynasty, and it was sourced from the *Abstracts of the Six Classics (Liu Yi Lue)* and the *Abstracts of the Works of Different Schools (Zhu Zi Lüe)*; the *Biography of Sima Rangju (Sima Rangju Zhuan)* and the *Biographies of Sun-Tzu and Wu Qi (Sun-Tzu Wu Qi Zhuan)* were sourced from the *Abstracts of the Books on Strategies for Wars (Bing Shu Lüe)*; the B*iographies of Qu Yuan and Master Jia (Qu Yuan Jia Sheng Zhuan)* and the *Biography of Sima Xiangru (Sima Xiangru Zhuan)* were sourced from the *Abstracts of the Poetries and Proses (Shi Fu Lüe)*, the *Biographies of Bian Que and Duke (Tai) Cang* was sourced from the *Abstracts of the Sciences and Witchcrafts (Fang Ji Lüe)*; the *Biographies of Diviners* and the *Biographies of Soothsayers* were sourced from the *Abstracts of the Works of Astrologers and Diviners (Shu Shu Lüe)*. In addition, the *Biographies of Usurers (Huo Zhi Zhuan)* mentioned social economy, while the *Biographies of the External Relatives (Wai Qi)* and *Biographies of Flatterers (Ning Xing Zhuan)* implied the causes for political disasters. All of these works are very insightful. On the other hand, it seems that the chapters were arranged for certain purpose. For example, the "royal annals" begin with the annals of Yao and Shun, while the "genealogies of noble houses" begin with the *House of Wu Taibo* and the "biographies" begin with the biography of Bo Yi, indicating the author's praise of comity and morality. This has been expounded by many people earlier so that it is not necessary to mention too many details here.

To read the *Records of the Grand Historian* for this purpose, it is better to read it from a high standard and an overall perspective. Do not only rigidly adhere to words and expressions. Then, the unique views which have formed a school of its own can be found.

The second is read it for purpose of study on ancient historical relics. The *Records of the Grand Historian* was the earliest general historical work. It has been used by many scholars as the basis for study on ancient historical relics. For this purpose, it is better to have an extensive reading of the book first and then find the key points of each period based on your own insights and read related content carefully. In this way, the essentials can be extracted to avoid excessive reading without summarization.

The third is to read it for study on writing skills. No one can deny the value of the articles in the *Records of the Grand Historian*. Moreover, for 2,000 years, the book has been read and studied by the later generations. It has become one of the classics for leaning common knowledge of the Chinese literature. Therefore, to learn literature, the book must be a basis. People who read the book for this purpose should carefully read ten masterpieces in the book. However, the selection of the masterpieces depends on the opinions of the readers. There is hardly any standard. For me, through all my life, I like the following chapters the most:

The *Annals of Xiang Yu (Xiang Yu Benji)*, the *Biography of the Lord of Xinling (Biography of the Prince of Wei)*, the *Biographies of Lian Po and Lin Xiangru*, the *Biographies of Lu Zhonglian and Zou Yang (Lu Zhonglian Zou Yang Liezhuan)*, the *Biography of the Marquis of Huaiyin, the Biographies of the Marquis of Weiqi and the Marquis of Wu'an (Weiqi Wu'an Hou Liezhuan), the Biography of General Li (Li Jiang Jun Liezhuan)*, the *Treatise on the Xiongnu*, the *Biographies of Usurers* and *The Preface of Shi Ji*.

These chapters boasting solemnness, inclusiveness and profound meaning set good examples for narrations. Ban Shupi had the following comments on Sima Qian: "He is a talented historian, who is good at narration, justification without rhetoric, simple and unsophisticated expression without vulgarness as well as direct and faithful record of history." The readers should read articles like them carefully to find the charm of the articles and the language and keep away from vulgarness and unreason.In the Ming and Qing dynasties, the *Biography of Bo Yi* (*Bo Yi Zhuan*), the *Biographies of Guan and Yan* (*Guan Yan Liezhuan*) and the *Biographies of Qu Yuan and Master Jia* became the favorites of many anthologists. However, in my opinion, these chapters belong to the second class.

The second way to read the *Records of the Grand Historian*

Let's continue the discussion about the ways to read the *Records of the Grand Historian*. It is an immortal classic masterpiece that should be read by everyone. However, it was so ancient that it is hard to understand; the names and features of things mentioned in the book have changed or become difficult to identify; there are many mistakes made in the process of copying the book. For these reasons, the book has been doubted or even disdained by people. So, less and less people would like to read it. It should be carefully compiled again so that more people would like it. I wish I can do it, but it is beyond my reach. What I can do is to tell you the ways I know. If any scholar can do it or several scholars can jointly do it, they will be crowned with eternal glory.

First, as mentioned above, the *Records of the Grand Historian* was supplemented and altered by the later generations. Therefore, it is better to make strict verification based on the earlier works on the book.In case of anything controversial, mark it with red line to avoid confusion with the original work. In this way, the

Former Residence of Liang Qichao

original text of the book can be verified. Scholars to devote themselves to such research may use the *Exploration to the Source of the Records of the Grand Historian* by Cui Shi as reference and make judgment based on their own researches.

Second, we attach great importance to the *Records of the Grand Historian* because that it recorded the history of the pre-Qin period. As to the history of the Qin and Han dynasties and the following dynasties, there are complete records in *The History of the Han Dynasty*. However, although there records of the history of the period under the reigns of Yao and Shun and that of the Xia, Shang and Zhou dynasties and the Spring and Autumn and the Warring States periods in other works, they cannot compare with the *Records of the Grand Historian*. Unfortunately, the records of the history of the pre-Qin period in the *Records of the Grand Historian* are not as sufficient as we have expected.

Regardless of the parts of the book supplemented and altered by the later generations, even the parts about the early history written by Sima Qian himself are not completely true. This should not be the responsibility of Sima Qian, because the histories of the ancient times are usually mixed with myths. Such phenomenon is shown worldwide, and there is no exception in China.

There used to be a lot of materials about the history of the ancient times, especially the Spring and Autumn and the Warring States periods. However, the Qin Empire ordered to burn the books and then many materials were lost. We believe that the defect of the book is not the lack of complete basis but the lack of elaborate verification and selection of materials. As Ban Shupi said, "The work by Sima Qian is based on wide range of historical materials and with penetration of the ancient classics, providing abundant information. However, a person has limited energy so that the book lacks sufficient basis and consistency and has some redundancies." (*The History of the Later Han Dynasty: the Bibliography of Ban Gu*).

By comparing the history of the pre-Qin period in the *Records of the Grand Historian* with books existing in this period, you will find that there are many redundancies and fabricated and fantastic stories in the book. Some chapters were conflict with each other. Even that, today, when writing histories about the ancient times, we still use the *Records of the Grand Historian* as a basis for verification. The scholars intending to be faithful to the work of Sima Qian should examine all the annals, genealogies and tables and collect circumstantial evidences and counter evidences from the book and other related works to prove and weed out the errors and maintain the essences of the book. The style of the *Commentaries on Romance of the Three Kingdoms* by Pei Songzhi can be adopted to make commentaries on each chapter to make the work well-grounded.

Scholars to devote to the research should use the *Verification of the Records of the Grand Historian (Shi Ji Zhi Yi)* by Liang Yusheng and *A Compilation of Traditional Classics Criticisms (Kao Xin Lu)* by Cui Shu as the major references. Then, the parts on the *Records of the Grand Historian* in the *Investigative Criticisms of the 22 Histories (Er Shi Er Shi Kao Yi)* by Qian Daxin, the *Reconsideration on Seventeen Histories (Shi Qi Shi Shang Que)* by Wang Mingsheng and the *Reading Notes on the Twenty-Two Histories (Er Shi Er Shi Zha Ji)* by Zhao Yi can be used as references. Finally, other reading notes and writings by the Confucian scholars of the Qing Dynasty can be used. However, it must be a complicated and heavy task that needs judgement and settlement of controversies. So, it will not be an easy job. Therefore, the success depends on the academic attainments and ability of judgement of the people engaged in it. Even so, people who are interested in the research may have a try with one or two chapters. Then, even if the result is not satisfying, the researchers can also benefit from the process with expanded knowledge of research methods and improved ethics.

III. The *Records of the Grand Historian* contains explanations, terms and descriptions that cannot be easily understood by the modern people. Therefore, annotations are needed. However, the early annotations are either too simple or too complicated so that deletion and supplement are needed. The best way to base on the questions of the modern middle school students to add concise annotations and make pauses in the unpunctuated ancient writings to make the book easy to read.

IV. The geographical information in the *Records of the Grand Historian* shows the positions of the historical sites and relics. However, many places have different names in the ancient and modern times. So, the readers may not know where the places are when reading the book. Therefore, it is better to prepare a catalogue of geographic names in both ancient and modern times.

V. The ancient China numbered the years in accordance with reigns of the emperors so that these years were hard to remember. In addition, during the Warring States period, different states had different ways of numbering the years, which were complicated and confusing. Therefore, it is better to prepare a chronology of events as supplement to the 10 tables in the book. The chronology should cover the whole history mentioned in the book and be numbered according to the western calendar, with remarks on related dynasties or states. It should start with the first year of Gonghe based on the *Yearly Chronicle of the Feudal Lords* and the events should be limited to those mentioned in the book.

The five points mentioned above compose an outline for systematic reading of the *Records of the Grand Historian*. The readers may adopt these ways to read the *Records of the Grand Historian* and even other works and will certainly and immeasurably benefit from the reading. It depends on the readers' will to study on which part of the book, for example, for comparison of political organizations or observation of social state.

Important references for study on the Records of the Grand
Historian: on three scholars' annotations on the Records of
the Grand Historian

Important references for study on the *Records of the Grand Historian*: on three scholars' annotations on the *Records of the Grand Historian*

Han Zhaoqi

The *Records of the Grand Historian* written by Sima Qian (145 to 90 B.C.?, the Western Han Dynasty) is a historical work that boasts broad conception and meticulous details. Meanwhile, it is also a great literary work with focus on people. It was first called *The Book of Taishigong* and later named the *Records of the Grand Historian* in the late Eastern Han Dynasty.

Three books of annotations on the *Records of the*

Grand Historian are the best-known, namely the *Collection of Annotations on the Records of the Grand Historian* by Pei Yin (Song Dynasty), the *Elucidation of the Records of the Grand Historian* by Sima Zhen (Tang Dynasty) and the *Correct Interpretation of the Records of the Grand Historian* by Zhang Shoujie (Tang Dynasty), which are the earliest and also the most important annotations on the *Records of the Grand Historian*.

The earliest annotations on the *Records of the Grand Historian* were made in the Eastern Han Dynasty. Yan Du wrote a volume of the *Pronunciation and Meaning of the Records of the Grand Historian (Shiji Yinyi)*, while someone wrote the five volumes of the *Elucidation of the Chapters of the Records of the Grand Historian (Shiji Zhangyin)*, which have been lost for a long time. In the Jin Dynasty, Xu Guang wrote another *Pronunciation and Meaning of the Records of the Grand Historian*, which provided basis for Pei Yin's *Collection of Annotations on the Records of the Grand Historian* but gradually lost with the popularity of the latter.

The *Collection of Annotations on the Records of the Grand Historian* by Pei Yin

Pei Yin, with the style name of Longju, was born in Wenxi, Hedong (currently northeast of Wenxi, Shanxi province) in the Song Dynasty. His father Pei Songzhi was famous as the author of the *Commentaries on Romance of* the Three Kingdoms (*San Guo Zhi Zhu*).Believing that the *Pronunciation and Meaning of the Records of the Grand Historian* was too simple, Pei Yin wrote the *Collection of Annotations on the Records of the Grand Historian*. Therefore, in addition to the almost all the content of Xu Guang's book, he also integrated a wide range of research results on the books related to the *Records of the Grand Historian* into his work, including the annotations on *The Commentary of Zuo* by Jia Kui, Fu Qian and Du Yu, the annotations on The History of the Han Dynasty by Ru Chun and Zhang Yan, the annotations on *The Discourses of the States* by Wei Shao, the annotations on *The Strategies of the Warring States* by Gao You, and the annotations on *The Analects of Confucius* by Kong Anguo and He Yan. Because that he collect the opinions of various scholars and made his own commentaries, he called the books "collections of annotations". He was so meticulous that he quoted the previous annotations with the name of the authors.

When writing the book, Pei Yin followed the principle of "annotating without questioning the original work", which was a traditional principle followed by the Confucians in the Han Dynasty. This led to obvious contrast between his work and the *Elucidation of the Records of the Grand Historian* by Sima Zhen. Even when finding errors in the narrations in the *Records of the Grand Historian*, Pei Yin usually just objectively quoted other sayings without any judgements by himself. For example,the *Biography of Lu Zhonglian(Lu Zhonglian Liezhuan)* said that, "more than 20 years after the (Event of Rescuing Handan), the general of Yan State took over Liaocheng through battles...Tian Dan of Qi State led the army to attack Liaocheng." Pei Yin quoted Xu Guang's words: "In accordance with the historical table, Tian Dan attacked Liaocheng 10 years after the Battle of Changping." However, in very rare cases, Pei Yin corrected the errors in the original text. For example, the *House of Chu (Chu Shijia)* said that, Prince Shangchen asked his teacher Pan Chong about how to know whether his father (Emperor Cheng of Chu) would abandon him and make his brother the prince. Pan Chong told him, "You should entertain the emperor's favorite concubine at banquet but do not respect her." Pei Yin annotated that "It should be the sister of the emperor instead of his concubine" in accordance with the annotations on *The Commentary of Zuo* by Du Yu, which said that: "You should entertain Jiang Mi but do not respect her." Du Yu annotated that: "Jiang Mi is Emperor Cheng of Chu's sister, who married a man of the Jiang's family."

The content of the *Collection of Annotations on the Records of the Grand Historian* is simple, too, also with errors. This is the major defect of the book. For example, the *Annals of Empress Dowager Lyu (Lyu Hou Benji)*said, "Prince Dai politely refused the invitation. Later, the envoy came again. Prince Dai finally accepted the invitation and went to the capital together with his fellows by six-horse carriage." Here, Pei Yin quoted Zhang Yan's annotations that, "It is also said that they wanted to ride horses to the capital after hearing about the change of the court." However, Dong Fen (Ming Dynasty) said that, "Six-horse carriage meant that it had been decided that the prince would take over the reign. It is the only way to invite him with the six-horse carriage. Zhang Yan was not right."

Following Pei Yin and his work, Zou Dansheng (Qi and Liang period) also wrote a *Pronunciation and Meaning of the Records of the Grand Historian*; in the Zhenguan

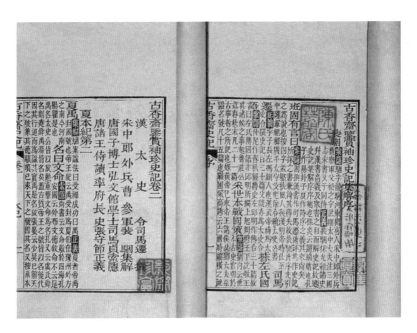

The *Records of the Grand Historian* with three scholars' annotations

period of the Tang Dynasty, Liu Bozhuang wrote another *Pronunciation and Meaning of the Records of the Grand Historian*, which consists of 20 volumes. The former had a few of annotations on pronunciations and little interpretation of meanings, while the latter had systematic annotations on pronunciations but less interpretation of meanings. Compared with that, the *Elucidation of the Records of the Grand Historian* by Sima Zhen contributes more to the researches on the *Records of the Grand Historian*.

The *Elucidation of the Records of the Grand Historian* by Sima Zhen

Sima Zhen, who lived in the Kaiyuan period of the Tang Dynasty, once worked as officials at the Imperial Academy and the Hongwen School and then as *Biejia* (official title) in Runzhou.

The style of the *Elucidation of the Records of the Grand Historian* is similar with that of the *Annotations to the Five Classics* (*Wu Jing Zhengyi*) by Kong Yingda. It contains annotations on the original text of the *Records of the Grand Historian* as well as annotations of the *Collection of Annotations on the Records of the Grand Historian* by Pei Yin. For example, the *Biographies of Qu Yuan and Master Jia* said that, "The *Book of Changes* said that 'The well has been cleared but still no one dare to drink the water'." The *Collection of Annotations on* the *Records of the Grand Historian* by Pei Yin quoted Xiang Xiu's words: "(Being) cleared means to get rid of the sludge." The *Elucidation of the Records of the Grand Historian* said that: "Xiang Xiu, with the style name of Zilang, lived in the Jin Dynasty. He wrote annotations on the *Book of Changes*."

Sima Zhen was wealthy in knowledge and talented. He didn't follow the principle of "annotating without questioning the original work", which was a traditional principle followed by the Confucians in the Han Dynasty. Instead, he studied on and corrected many errors in the *Collection of Annotations on the Records of the Grand Historian* by Pei Yin. For example, the *Treatise on the Eastern Yue* (*Dong Yue Liezhuan*) mentions the place named "Meiling". The *Collection of Annotations on the Records of the Grand Historian* quoted Xu Guang's explanation and said, "Meiling is in Kuaiji." However, the *Elucidation of the Records of the Grand Historian* said, "Xu Guang made a mistake. Meiling is in Yuzhang." There is another example. The *House of Jin* (*Jin Shijia*) said, "Xun Linfu served as the Middle General, while Xiangu served as the Right General and Xianmie served as the Left General." The *Collection of Annotations on the Records of the Grand Historian* quoted the explanations of Du Yu, "The three forces had no generals. It may refer to commander." However, the *Elucidation of the Records of the Grand Historian* said, "In accordance with *The*

Commentary of Zuo, Xun Linfu was a minister. So it must not refer to commander. There was no general because of the taboo of the emperor. Therefore, the system of three forces was adopted, with the titles of these forces unknown." These annotations just stick to the quick. Sima Zhen not only contradicted some annotations by Xu Guang and Pei Yin, but also raised doubts about the original text written by Sima Qian and provided opinions on the identification of the errors and correction. For example, the *Biographies of Confucian Scholars* said that, "Confucius applied for positions with more than 70 state leaders but was refused." The *Elucidation of the Records of the Grand Historian* said, "The later recorder of the history must have made a mistake. The *Homely Talk (Jia Yu)* said that Confucius visited a number of small states seeking for a chance for a position. There is no mentioning of 'more than 70 states'." They are incisive and new elucidations.

Sima Zhen not only find the errors in the original text of the *Records of the Grand Historian*, but also made amendment and supplement.For example, he believed that the chapter about Xian Yu should be classified into genealogies and the chapter about Chen She should be classified into biographies, and there should be chapters about Zichan and Shuxiang. He even wrote the *Annals of the Three Emperors (San Huang Benji)* and put it behind the *Annals of the Five Emperors*. However, some amendments and supplements reflect different views and too keen-edged argument, seeming to be redundant.

The *Elucidation of the Records of the Grand Historian* also include some errors. For example, concerning the *House of Wu Taibo*, which said that Prince Geyu and Prince Zhuyong were sent to besiege the Lu and Qian towns,the *Elucidation of the Records of the Grand Historian* said, "*The Spring and Autumn Annals* mentioned Prince Yanyu, while the *Records of the Grand Historian* mentioned him as Geyu. That may be because that Sima Qian disliked the character of "Yan" (homophone to castration in Chinese) after suffering the castration." Liang Yusheng refuted, "Sima Qian had never cared for the character of 'Yan'. He used it for many times in other chapters of the book." Obviously, the elucidation of Sima Zhen was too superficial.

Sima Zhen was very talented and made great achievements through the *Elucidation of the Records of the Grand Historian*, which was paralleled with Yan Shigu's *Annotations on The History of the Han Dynasty* by the Mao Jin, a famous bibliophile living in the late Ming and early Qing dynasties.

Besides the two works mentioned above, there is another important work on the *Records of the Grand Historian*, namely Zhang Shoujie's *Correct Interpretation of the Records of the Grand Historian*, which was finished slightly later after the *Elucidation of the Records of the*

Grand Historian.

The *Correct Interpretation of the Records of the Grand Historian* by Zhang Shoujie

Zhang Shoujie also lived in the Kaiyuan period of the Tang Dynasty, later than Sima Zhen. He once accompanied several princes studying at school and served as *Xuanyilang* (official title) and head of aides and staff of princes. The *Correct Interpretation of the Records of the Grand Historian* was finished in the 24th year of the Kaiyuan Period (736).

The book includes annotations on the original text of the *Records of the Grand Historian* as well as annotations on the *Collection of Annotations on the Records of the Grand Historian* and the *Elucidation of the Records of the Grand Historian*. There have been no controversies on that the *Correct Interpretation of the Records of the Grand Historian* made annotations on the former two works mentioned above. However, concerning the annotations on the *Elucidation of the Records of the Grand Historian*, the controversies was not settled until 1962, when the research results of Cheng Jinzao was published. For example, the *Annals of Qin (Qin Benji)* said, "In the 24th year under the reign of the Duke Xiao of Qin State, (Qin's army) fought against the Jin's army at Yanmen." The *Elucidation of the Records of the Grand Historian* said, "The *Annals (Ji Nian)* said that (it) fought against the Wei's

Important references for study on the Records of the Grand
Historian: on three scholars' annotations on the Records of
the Grand Historian

The *Records of the Grand Historian*

army at Anmen. Here, the 'Yanmen' should be a mistake. The text below also said that (it) defeated Han's army at Anmen. So, it should be the same place. The wars against the Han's and Wei's armies should not occur at Yanmen, which was too far away." The *Correct Interpretation of the Records of the Grand Historian* said, "*Comprehensive Geography (Kuo Di Zhi)* said that Anmen is 28 li far away from Changshe County of Xuzhou on the northwest, and is named Xiwuting today." There is another example. The *Annals of Xiang Yu* said, "Liu Gu's army massacred all residents of Chengfu and then arrived at Gaixia." The *Elucidation of the Records of the Grand Historian* said, "The *San Cang Zhu* by Zhang Yi said that Gai refers to a dyke in Pei Prefecture."The *Correct Interpretation of the Records of the Grand Historian* said, "Gaixia refers to a cliff at Gaogang, about three or four *zhang* (a unit of length). Both the city and dyke mentioned sit at its side so that it was named Gaixia. It is 10 li far away from the current Zhenyuan County, Haozhou, adjoining the Laojun Temple."

Zhang Shoujie was good at geography and made great contribution in geographical study. He refuted some incorrect annotations in the book. For example, the *House of Wei (Wei Shijia)* said, "The prince fought against the Qi's army and was defeated at Maling." The *Collection of Annotations on the Records of the Grand Historian* quoted Xu Guang's words: "It should be at Yuancheng."

Important references for study on the Records of the Grand
Historian: on three scholars' annotations on the Records of
the Grand Historian

The *Correct Interpretation of the Records of the Grand Historian* said, "*Maling* is 60 li far away from Juancheng County of Puzhou on the northeast. How could the Qi's army defeat the Wei's army at Maling in the process of marching to Daliang? So, Xu Guang made a mistake."

However, the *Correct Interpretation of the Records of the Grand Historian* also has some errors. For example, the *Biographies of Assassins* said, "The story of Jing Ke happened 220 years later." The *Collection of Annotations on the Records of the Grand Historian* corrected it: "From Nie Zheng to Jing Ke, there were 70 years." The *Correct Interpretation of the Records of the Grand Historian* said, "From the First Emperor of the Qin Dynasty to Marquis Ai, there were 643 years."Moreover, the biggest defect of the *Correct Interpretation of the Records of the Grand Historian* is it includes too many contents that are not necessary. For example, the *Annals of the Xiaowen Emperor* (Xiaowen Benji) mentioned Gaoling, which were annotated with more than 150 Chinese characters, including 120 characters that are unnecessary.

Therefore, when being copied and printed later, the book was abridged optionally. That's why different versions of the book have different contents. It is a phenomenon that was rarely seen among other annotation works.

The *Collection of Annotations on the Records of the Grand Historian*, the *Elucidation of the Records of the Grand Historian* and the *Correct Interpretation of*

A Still of film named *The Emperor and the Assassin*

the Records of the Grand Historian have close relations, usually the latter making annotations for the former. However, the *Collection of Annotations on the Records of the Grand Historian* was attached to the original text of the *Records of the Grand Historian*, while the *Elucidation of the Records of the Grand Historian* and the *Correct Interpretation of the Records of the Grand Historian* are independent works. In the Song Dynasty, some people tried to integrate the annotations in the three works into the notes below the original text of the *Records of the Grand Historian*. Unfortunately, the carving copy of the book of this type by Huang Shanfu (during the Qingyuan period under the reign of Emperor Ningzong of the Southern

Song Dynasty) was lost. The currently popular version of the *Records of the Grand Historian* in the *Twenty-Four Histories* (collection of various editions) was edited based on that. The version with integrated annotations from the three books, which is convenient for reading, has been the favorite version of the readers for 700 years. The version reedited with punctuations and published by Zhonghua Book Company in 1959 is also based on that. It is very popular now.

Martyrdom and transcendence: on the tragic spirits under the *Records of the Grand Historian*

Han Zhaoqi & Wang Qi

More and more researchers have reached the consensus that the *Records of the Grand Historian* is a great work with tragic color, which cultured tragic spirit that, to a large extent, generates the energy to shock and excite the readers. Here, the tragic spirit means the extraordinary disposition and noble and outstanding moral characters shown by the people recorded in the book when they were suffering and fighting against tragic fate. It was mainly manifested in the following aspects.

I. the spirit of martyrdom

The spirit of martyrdom refers to a kind of passion to life that makes the tragic people to sacrifice themselves. Based on the study on the Greek tragedy, Marx believed that the tragic people had such spirit. He said, "Prometheus is the most noble saint and martyr in the philosophy books." (See Volume II, *Karl Marx and Friedrich Engels on Literature and Art*) Most of the tragic people under the *Records of the Grand Historian* had the ideal and pursuit of sacrificing themselves to benefit the mankind and the society and making successes. For example, Confucius, who drifted from place to place and suffered many disasters through his life, had been insisting on his ideal and faith so that he could safeguard and spread the truth that he believed through his ascetic practices. Qu Yuan, who, with indignation, committed suicide by drowning himself in the Miluo River, manifested the spirit of martyrdom of the Chinese intellectuals with his life. Bo Yi and Shu Qi starved themselves to death to safeguard the righteousness. Wang Zhu cut his own throat after the invaders occupied his country. In addition, Jing Ke, Yu Rang as well as Tian Heng and his 500 guests also showed the religious devotion and sacrifice spirit to some extent. They sacrificed themselves for different reasons, some for their nation, while some for certain faith or righteousness. There were differences in their sacrifice. However, their enthusiasm and devotion and spirit of self-sacrifice were beyond the desire for gain usually held by the common people and showed the spirit of selflessness and fearlessness to pursue for the righteousness, regardless of how the world people dreamed of gains.

Among the tragic people with the spirit of martyrdom, there were also people like Shang Yang and Chao Cuo who were inescapability forced to sacrifice themselves to the human progress. Shang Yang's reform enabled the Qin State to go toward prosperity and laid a foundation for China's unity in the future. Chao Cuo's policy to weaken the vassal states was the only way to consolidate the empire of Han at that time; otherwise, there should be a historical retrogression. What they did must benefit the later generations. However, the reality decided that their sacrifice is an inevitable result. Their sacrifice just reflected their excellent qualities as martyrs. Marx said that, "Among the human beings, like that in the world of animals and plants, the interests of a racial group are always gained by sacrificing some individuals' interests. The reason for it is the consistency of the interests of the racial group and some special individuals, who just have the power and superiority." Therefore, it is always that people with the spirit of martyrdom play the role as that it is their duty to sacrifice. Also, it is because of the everlasting spirit of martyrdom, the human beings gained the passion to get out of the abyss of the desire for gains.

Tian Heng and His 500 Guests by Xu Beihong

II. The spirit of suspicion

Most of the tragic people were good at introspection and suspicion. They were not reconciled or reluctant to admit the prescriptiveness of the reality. We call such spirit the "spirit of suspicion".

The tragic people with the spirit of suspicion usually lived with confusion and pain of complaints, because they could not understand and bear the suffering and sadness in their life but they could not explain or face up to the right and root reasons for that due to the restriction of the times or the world views. For example, in the *Biography of General Li*, General Li Guang did not get the treatment as he deserved, though he spent his whole life in fighting for the great Han Empire. Some military officers who made less contributions than Li did were promoted to higher positions. So, he sadly asked the fortune-teller, "Am I doomed to have no fortune to become a marquis?" He suspected and not reconciled to the fate so that he recommended himself for a battle. After he was refused, he became very angry with Wei Qin. Finally, he committed suicide after being marginalized for a long time. There is another example. Bai Qi, a renowned general of the Qin Dynasty, showed his suspicion and grief when he was coerced into committing suicide by the emperor even though he did not do anything wrong. He asked, "How can they treat me like this? I am innocent." That's just what General Meng Tian said when he was framed.Nakai

Sekitoku said when reading about the suicide of General Bai Qi, "He said so when he was forced to committing suicide because he knew that he was innocent. It is the same with Meng Tian." (Takigawa Sukenobu, *Research and Supplement to the Annotations of the Records of the Grand Historian*). Other officials who also suffered defamation and traps, such as Long Feng, Bi Gan, Qu Yuan and Wu Zixu, all had suspicions on the fatuous and self-indulgent rulers who gave them unfair treatment. On the other hand, the brutality and the illusions of the world also made people doubtful of the efforts and struggles they had made through their short life, especially when people set the pursuit of benefits as the foundation of their lives. In the *Biography of Li Si*, stimulated by the observation of the mouse, young Li Si devoted themselves to pursuing riches and honors. However, he was finally cut in two at the waist. Before his death, he said to his son, "I want to hunt rabbits together with you and our yellow dog outside the east gate of Shangcai. We will never have the chance anymore!" This also shows his suspicion on the significance of riches and honors to his life. He even denied the value of his life. Even the most steadfast martyrs, such as Confucius, sometimes showed confusions on the disorder of the world. He once asked himself and his students, "Could there be Bo Yi's and Shu Qi's suffering if anyone with kindheartedness is believed; could there be Bi Gan's suffering if any wise man goes smoothly on his road."

(House of Confucius). It is just the spirit of suspicion that leads to Sima Qian's suspicion and confusion on the nature, the people and the social conditions.

III. The spirit of anti-moderation

The Confucian school has been emphasizing the charm of "moderation". *The Analects of Confucius* said, "Moderation is the highest virtue." Concerning art, through the history of literature that began with *The Book of Songs (Shi Jing)*, the literature circle has been embracing the tradition of "enjoying without indulgence and deeply feeling but not sentimental". Concerning the personality, tenderness and gentleness have been highly praised. However, with the passion to directly face the life, Sima Qian exposed the cruelty of the society. The tragic figures in his book unbosomed their inner voices and grief and indignation, which revealed their untrammeled personalities and the cruelty of the society. Such spirit to directly face the life is called the spirit of anti-moderation.

Ban Gu once made veiled criticism of the *Records of the Grand Historian*. He said, "Its views on the right and wrong are some contrary to the sages, and it gives priority to philosophies of the Yellow Emperor and Lao-Tzu rather than the six classics. It talks more about the knight-errants than the hermits and excuses the ambitious careerists. It talks about the usurers and speaks high of the people of great influence and shames the poor and the lower class."

班令史

Portrait of Ban Gu

(*The History of the Han Dynasty: the Biography of Sima Qian*) Such criticism from the perspective of orthodox Confucianism just reflects the spirit of anti-moderation in Sima Qian's work. Most of the tragic people in the *Records of the Grand Historian* had extraordinarily untrammeled personalities and circumstances of life.Confucius believed that Bo Yi and Shu Qi set a good example for people without complaints and blame. He said, "They sought virtue and acquired it. What to complain about?" However, in the *Records of the Grand Historian*, they became the first to blame the leader's way of governance by replacing one tyranny by another and firmly separated themselves from the society in an uncompromising way. Even when they were starved to death, they said, "Let's climb up the western hill to pick the wild plants. The emperor who replaced one tyranny by another cannot realize it is a mistake. The world of peace and prosperity established by Shennong, Shun and Yu has been lost. Where's our home? Oh, the only way is to die. How unfortunate we are!" Was that not a complaint? Therefore, Li Zhi said in his *Burning Books* (*Fen Shu*), "Confucius said there is no complaint, while Sima Qian said there are complaints. It is the complaints made the work fine and ingenious." (*Burning Book*, Volume 5). The characters in the *Biographies of Assassins* (*Ci Ke Liezhuan*) and the *Biographies of Knight-errants*, including Jing Ke, Nie Zheng, Yu Rang, Zhu Jia and Guo Jie, whose behaviors were against the righteousness and the principle of tenderness and gentleness, kept their promises and never stopped their actions until success was achieved, even that they had to sacrifice their lives. These people usually had a strong sense of justice and were ready to help the weak by force. They did not care their lives but attached great importance to the righteousness. They were not restricted by traditional morality. It also reflects the spirit of anti-moderation.

The characters with the spirit of anti-moderation in the *Records of the Grand Historian* dared to fight against the fate or the limitation of the prescriptiveness of the reality to realize the value of their lives as far as possible. They defied the political power and expected successes. They would like to take actions to fight against the bad fate, even at the expense of their lives. For example, Chen Sheng, who did not yield to the fate and the racial and familial suppression, rose in revolt against the tyranny of rulers of the Qin Dynasty. He said, "Do the noble doomed to be noble?" It just the declaration of anti-moderation. Wu Zixu turned the fire of rebel toward the fatuous king; General Li Guang committed suicide after experiencing the coercion and marginalization of the relatives of the imperial family. What these people did was driven by their personality of resistance. People with the spirit of anti-moderationhad never been satisfied with their lives so that they had been advancing bravely through the adversities, which revealed their extreme discordance with the reality. To the largest extent, the tragic spirit reflects the pursuits of the people for freedom and an extraordinary life. It has the greatest driving power.

Lu Xun said, "Tragedy is to destroy the valuable thing and show it." Sima Qian incisively and vividly showed how the humanness, beauty, kindness and dignity of the people in the history were unmercifully trampled. This makes the *Records of the Grand Historian* a unique collection of tragedies manifesting the spirit of anti-moderation in the history. In accordance with the book, many good people had a tragic end. For example, Ji Ci and Yuan Xian lived a poor life and died early (*Biographies of Knight-errants*). Bo Yi and Shu Qi starved themselves to death (*Biography*

Portrait of Lu Xun

of Bo Yi). Qu Yuan was doubted and defamed and finally drowned himself in a river. Wu Zixu's body was put into a leather bag and thrown into the river after he died, because he told the truth to King Fuchai. Many characters in the book were fragile and indifferent. Concubine Qi was punished with arms and legs cut off and body badly damaged under the order of Empress Lyu. The hero Xiang Yu allowed his fellow townsmen to separate his body after his death to get the rewards from his enemies. The book show a world with greediness for benefits, pursuit for power, loveless marriage for political purposes and cold-blooded relationships among family members. It is full of poignant sarcasms and ridicule to the political leaders as well as discontent and indignation about the unfair social system. Just as Li Changzhi said, "The tradition of 'enjoying without indulgence and deeply feeling but not sentimental' was changed by Sima Qian into 'being joyous or sad as you want'. We can hear the real voices of the people in the book."(*Personalities and Style of Sima Qian*) .

IV. The spirit of swallowing humiliation and bearing a heavy task

The tragic heroes under the *Records of the Grand Historian* all have indomitable vitality. They never gave up any chances for their self-fulfillment and sought for survival at any cost, whether it was humiliation, damage, strike or inherent painful suffering, as long as it was not death. The traffic people wished to be crowned with eternal glory in the future so that they all tried hard to make their life significant. That's why Sima Qian said in *A Letter to Ren An* that, "I swallowed the humiliation and lived on in degradation because that I still have the selfish motives to let my work known to the later generations." We call this the spirit of swallowing humiliation and bearing a heavy task. For example, after being punished with kneecaps removed under the order of Pang Juan, Sun Bin left the Wei State on the excuse of the state could not provide him the chances to realize one's aspirations and became a general of the Qi State. Then, the army led by Sun Bin defeated the army of the Wei State. Sun Bin became widely well-known and his book of strategies for wars was widely spread. (Biographies of Sun Tzu and Wu Qi) King Gou Jian, after being defeated, slept on the brushwood and tasted the gall every day to undergo self-imposed hardships so as to strengthen his resolve to revenge. He took the lead to do farm work for self-sufficiency and make friends with talents. Finally, his army dominated the Wu State (*House of King Goujian of Yue*). Fan Ju was mistaken for spy of the enemy state when he served as an official of the Wei State. He was badly beat, with ribs and teeth broken, and then thrown into toilet. The drunk guests peed on his body to insult him. However, he finally escaped to the Qin State and became a prime minister of the Qin State with great contributions. He finally revenged to wipe out a humiliation (*Biographies of Fan Ju*).

These people, with great persistence, tried to seize the smallest chance in their tragic life to make success or another glory in the life.

The heroes who bit the bullet, with their extraordinary toughness, endured the suffering and humiliation that ordinary people can hardly bear. It not only won the compassion of the other people, but also their respect. Such spirit just corresponds to the saying that suffering makes heroes. Just as Mencius said, "When Heaven is about to place a great responsibility on a great man, it always first frustrates his spirit and will, exhausts his muscles and bones, exposes him to starvation and poverty, harasses him by troubles and setbacks so as to stimulate his spirit, toughen his nature and enhance his abilities." The stories about how Han Xin and other unfortunate talents endured humiliation and then made great successes are very moving, and the traffic spirit of swallowing humiliation and bearing a heavy task has been embraced in the Chinese culture and philosophical consciousness.

V. The spirit of transcendence

In the *Annals of Xiang Yu*, Sima Qian described such a scene: Xiang Yu was pushed by Liu Bang's army to the wall. His lover had died and his army had been routed, only with 28 cavalrymen left. There was a small boat at the riverside. Xiang Yu should have the chance to take the boat back to Jiangdong, where he could linger out his life (or

Xiang Yu

try to bob up like a cork). However, he did not do that. He
accepted the destiny for a tragic end in an extremely traffic
way. Although he knew that he was doomed to fail, he still
tried to challenge the destiny. He led the 28 cavalrymen
to fight against the enemies for the last time. He stared at
the enemies, not caring about the hopeless future nut just
enjoying the glory and vitality as a victor at that moment.
At that time, his heroic, pride dignity and fearless courage
transcended the incoming tragedy. He said loudly, "I know
that I am doomed to fail, but I am not failed now. I will
only lose to the intangible 'heaven', but not the enemies."
Finally, he cut off his own head to prove that it was his
own choice to die and neither the 'heaven' nor any other
forces defeated him. In a sense, Xiang Yu was a warrior
that completely won. His spirit will never die.

The *Annals of Xiang Yu* has been recognized as the best chapter under the *Records of the Grand Historian* (*Personalities and Style of Sima Qian*). It is also one of the chapters with the most highlighted tragic spirits. As Albert Camus said, "Say 'yes' to life, but say 'no' to the future." (*The Myth of Sisyphus*) We call it the spirit of transcendence to maintain sincere desire in desperation, seek permanent advance in absolute failure and enrich the value of life in a dark world. The spirit of transcendence does not mean that people should resign themselves to adversity or do nothing. It is to hold on to fight to the end (*Robert W. Corrigan, Tragedy and the Tragic Spirit*, quoted from *On Tragic and Comic Spirits*). The spirit of transcendence is also purifying spirit that turns the sense of tragedy to the sense of loftiness. It leads people to release themselves from the suffering and failure to face and contend against the tragedy and step toward high spirit and enthusiasm.

The spirit of transcendence is usually highlighted in destruction and failure. It serves as a solid protective screen for people's dignity and nobleness, enabling people to maintain some pride no matter how humble they are so that they will never be defeated. Many of the characters under the *Records of the Grand Historian*, such as Xiang Yu, Li Guang and Wu Zixu, were proud and undefeatable. They never compromised to the reality. Instead, they tries to prove their value even at the expense of life. Therefore, they showed great courage and the heroic spirit and passion.

Of course, the tragic spirits mentioned above are just part of the tragic elements under the *Records of the Grand Historian*. However, they are the most prominent representatives of the tragic spirits indicated by the book, showing the concepts and attitudes of the tragic characters toward the nature, fate, life, society and individuals. The tragedy of Sima Qian plays a leading role among these tragic spirits, which faithfully reflect the spiritual state of the people through the history amidst the winds of change. The tragic spirits make the suffering people noble ones and enhance the value and charm of the *Records of the Grand Historian* in the journey of the human beings to seek the truth.

The *Records of the Grand Historian* and the biographical literature of ancient China

Han Zhaoqi

China has a long history of a good development of historical proses. Existing written works prove that the earliest historical prose appeared in the Shang Dynasty, named *Pan Geng*, which was followed by *Da Gao*, *Mu Shi* and *Wu Yi*, which are all parts of *The Book of Documents*. In addition, there are *The Discourses of the States*, *The Commentary of Zuo* and *The Strategies of the Warring State*, which appeared in the Spring and Autumn and Warring States periods. Some of these works are in annalistic style, for the purpose of making records; some of them were arranged by country, most for recording opinions, or even some like collections of data. They represent certain achievements in plots and structure, description of scene and psychological expression. However, by the times mentioned above, the so-called biographic works centering people had not appeared.

The *Records of the Grand Historian* by Sima Qian is the first biographical work on the history and literature stages. It is the formal beginning as well as the most excellent representative of the biographical literature of ancient China. It sets an example for and has great influence on the ancient Chinese biographical proses and novels. Hereunder, it will be interpreted from the following aspects.

First, no historical records and related literatures can be comparable with the *Records of the Grand Historian* in terms of the faithfulness to the history. Sima Qian has outstanding matter-of-fact attitude so that he widely collected, verified and selected historical materials. To write the book, he read the books in the imperial library and archives, and nearly travelled through the whole country and took any chances to visit the historic relics and traces. This enabled him to accumulate abundant knowledge, expand his horizon, greatly improve his ideological awareness and enhance his ability to identify problems.

Liu Bang

Even with the abilities to identify the facts and make right judgement on what is right or wrong, without enough courage, the author could not faithfully show it to the readers. That's why Sima Qian is respected. He clearly approved and praised what he believed should be approved and praised regardless of whether the ruling class like it or not. Actually, many of his opinions went against the official consensus. For example, many people at that time did not believe that the Qin Dynasty that was overturned by Liu Bang was a real dynasty. They believed the Zhou Dynasty was directly followed by the Han Dynasty. However, Sima Qian had different opinions. He first wrote the two royal annals about the Qin Dynasty and its first emperor, and then bitterly rebuked people who flattered Liu Bang and denied the fact that Qin was a dynasty in the *Yearly Chronicle of the Six States*. There is another example. Although the death of knight-errant Guo Xie was related to Emperor Wu of Han Dynasty, Sima Qian still glorified him regardless of the threat to his own life. How hard it was! In addition, the courage of Sima Qian to tell the truth is also reflected by his tries to not the change the fact due to what he himself liked and disliked.For example, obviously, Sima Qian disliked Wu Qi, Shang Yang, Liu Bang and Empress Dowager Lyu. However, he faithfully recorded their abilities and successes in the book. Although he liked Wu Zixu, Xiang Yu and Li Guang, he faithfully talked about their weaknesses in personality, which decided that they must get a tragic end finally. That's why the *Records of the Grand Historian* was highly praised by Liu Xiang, Yang Xiong, Ban Gu and other historians and scholars, who said that, "The work boasts justification without rhetoric, simple and unsophisticated expression without vulgarness as well as direct and faithful record of history". Ban Gu once expressed his dissatisfaction with the *Records of the Grand Historian*. Even so, he also prodigally praised it.

Lu Xun said, "Generally satires are about the facts; otherwise, it does not constitute sarcasm."It is the same to see the criticalness of the *Records of the Grand Historian*. To a large extent, the book revealed the real society of the Han Dynasty and exposed many shameful secrets

and darkness inside the ruling class. That's why Sima
Qian was hated by Emperor Wu of Han Dynasty and the
contemporary nobles, and even criticized by many later
"orthodox" scholars, who said his book was a slanderous
book. Actually, due to various reasons, Sima Qian indeed
showed some extreme opinions on a number of issues.
However, to a historian, the courage to face the truth,
expose the conflicts and write down the truth is extremely
valuable. He was castrated just because he directly told
the truth; because he wrote *A Letter to Ren An*, he got the
end with unknown death. Also, for this, Sima Qian became
a unique benchmark in the history that no one can go
beyond. After Sima Qian, there were almost no historians
to make records of contemporary history. Usually, the
historians of the Tang Dynasty wrote about the history
of the Song Dynasty, while that of the Song Dynasty
wrote about the history of the Yuan Dynasty, and so on. In
addition, in most cases, the courts organized the historians
to write histories. Therefore, it is nothing strange that
the historical records cannot reflect the opinions and
expectations of the authors.

There are less truths and criticalness in the official
history books. Even though, single-chapter biographical
literatures had a development. For example, there are the
Biography of Sir Wu Liu (Wu Liu Xian Sheng Zhuan) by
Tao Yuanming, the *Autobiography of Liu Yuxi (Ziliuzi Zi
Zhuan)* by Liu Yuxi and the *A Record for Five Men's Tomb*

(*Wu Ren Mu Bei Ji*) by Zhang Pu. The former two works write about the authors themselves, while the latter one is about people of the same time. Although these works are about individuals and individual events, they touches many important contemporary issues in political and socials customs, showing strong awareness of fighting against the reality. In this aspect, they remain the connections with the thoughts and spirits contained in the *Records of the Grand Historian*.

Second, historical books are not just records of history. They are the way for the authors to show their ideals and create the philosophies of their own. In *A Letter to Ren An*, Sima Qian revealed his purposes to write the book, "I am trying to do something beyond my ability to use my insufficient writing skills to collect historical materials nationwide, briefly verify the facts and tell the truth, trying to find the reasons for the successes and failures as well as the prosperity and decline...It is also purpose to explore the relationship between the nature and the human society and show the historical changes through the ages, and to create the philosophy of my own." What does it mean to create the philosophy of one's own? Liang Qichao explained that, "It was the same thing that drove Sima Qian to write the *Records of the Grand Historian*, Xun Kuang to write the *Hsun-Tzu,* Dong Zhongshu to write the *Luxuriant Dew of the Spring and Autumn Annals (Chun Qiu Fan Lu)*, namely to form up their own philosophies

Langya Stone Inscription of Qin Dynasty

through the historical works. Therefore, it is hard to really understand the *Records of the Grand Historian* if it is only read based on the modern concepts." (*Interpretations of the Classics and Ways of Reading, Yao Ji Jie Ti Ji Qi Du Fa*) This is the opinion from an overall perspective. Taking the example of the single chapters, Sima Qian just wrote about the individuals and the individual events. Many earlier scholars had such consensus. Chen Renxi (the Ming Dynasty) said, "Sima Qian wrote every biography with a purport." Gao Buying, a modern scholar, said that, "Every chapter by Sima Qian has its own purport. For example, the *House of Wu Taibo* focuses on 'comity' and 'scramble'; the *House of Lu Zhougong (Lu Zhougong Shijia)* focuses on the contributions of Zhougong; the *House of Chancellor Chen (Chen Chengxiang Shijia)* focuses on conspiracies; the Biographies of the Marquis of Weiqi and the Marquis of Wu'an focuses on the sorption of power and influence; the *Treatise on the Dayuan (Dayuan Liezhuan)* focuses on communication and military development, with the former part about the communication through the envoys based on the journey of Zhang Qian and the latter part about the military development based on the development of the horses of Dayuan." The summaries of the purports of the chapters under the *Records of the Grand Historian* may be not authoritative, because everyone has different understanding of them. However, it is no denying that every chapter has a purport. The purports of some chapters are especially clear. For example, the *Annals of the Five Emperors* was written to praise abdication and the concept to deem the whole world as one community; the *Biography of the Prince of Wei* was written to praise the behavior to be courteous to the wise and condescending to scholars and criticize the fatuous ruler for destroying the Great Wall; the *Biography of the Marquis of Huaiyin* was written to reveal the cruel actions of the ancient imperial rulers to kill the meritorious after they took the reign. Through the book, Sima Qian showed what he was pursuing for and what he hated and cursed.

Sima Qian wrote about his ideal in a way to tell the true history and show the development rules rather than adding anything into the history. The more typical and profound the facts and rules are, the more significant they are in constituting contrast with the real society and education. Therefore, the author did not have to give any hints and the readers will make associations. For example, concerning the failure of the Qin Dynasty, Sima Qian wrote, "The emperor (referring to the First Emperor of the Qin Dynasty) was cruel and self-righteous. He used to be a duke and then unified the country so that he believed that no one can compare with him throughout the history. He laid particular stress on prison officers... The prime minister and other ministers had to execute his orders without doubt. The emperor liked to establish authority with heavy punishment so that no officials dared to tell the truth." He also wrote, "The expostulation made by the officials were deemed as defamation. Therefore, the officials only fawn on the emperor to keep their positions. The people were shocked and frightened." This reminds us of the situation during the reign of Emperor Wu of Han Dynasty. It said that, "(The emperor) was indulged in expansion through wars and an extravagant life, which were at the expense of frequent wars and great consumption of resources. Under such a circumstance, the people lived a poor life and crimes increased. The cruel officials held the power of sentence, but crimes could not be stopped. Therefore, Zhang Jin and Zhao Yu were designated to make laws, which stipulated that the supervision officials should be punished if they knew the crimes but did not report it and the officials who imposed a lenient sentence on the criminals or even released the criminals should be sentenced to death immediately." *Dasinong* (official title) Yan Yi was even charged of "unspoken criticism" and killed. Several prime ministers who held the position in succession during the late reign of Emperor Wu of Han Dynasty were killed so that no one dared to hold the position. Therefore, "the officials covered crimes for each other and made false documents to avoid legal responsibilities". "The senior officials were not capable for their positions. They just tried to behave and speak carefully to avoid making mistakes and keep their positions." What shocking facts! The typical and insightful

Photocopy of Selected Works of The *Strategies of the Warring States*

writing skills of the author made these facts permanent lessons and warnings. This is one of the major factors for the charm of the *Records of the Grand Historian*. The characteristic of the book to show the ideal of the author was inherited by many latter authors of miscellaneous biographies, such as Han Yu, who wrote the *Biography of Carpenters* (*Zi Ren Zhuan*), Liu Zongyuan, who wrote the B*iography of Guo Tuotuo Who Planting Trees* (*Zhong Shu Guo Tuotuo Zhuan*), and Su Shi, who wrote the *Biography of Fang Shanzi* (*Fang Shanzi Zhuan*). The former two biographies are about the lower class. Whether there were really the people mentioned in these works are unknown. The latter one is about a person named Chen Zao but has no relations with the society and life. All these works highlight the ideals of the authors toward the society and the philosophies for life and the social conducts. They focus more on reasoning than the characters themselves. Such kind of works inherit the characteristics of the *Biography of Bo Yi* and the *Biographies of Soothsayers* under the *Records of the Grand Historian*.

Third, when writing the book, the author focused on the description of the characters and the personalities and typicality of the characters rather than whether the information was sufficient and complete. At that time, there was no clear boundary between historical works and literature. Sima Qian tried to reach the peak whether in historical works or literature. He was not satisfied with the chronological structure of *The Commentary of Zuo* and the miscellaneous compilation of *The Discourses of the States* and *The Strategies of the Warring States*. What he wanted is to create a historical work presented in a series of biographies, with the annals of the emperors as the general guideline and the genealogies of noble houses and biographies as details. With his utmost efforts, he built a vivid and splendid "gallery" of historical figures for the later generations. It was a period with great social instability, reforms, wars and pains from the Warring States period to the Han Dynasty, but was also a period with magnificent upsurges and heroes coming forth in large numbers and getting the chances to make great accomplishments. Therefore, what the *Records of the Grand Historian* shows to us is not only a gallery of historical figures, but also a gallery of heroes, especially tragic heroes. Sima Qian applied and innovated the descriptive methods used in the historical biographies of the pre-Qin period to depict these tragic heroes, reaching a new level in creation of historical works. That's why there are so many vivid and distinctive characters (such as Wu Zixu, Lin Xiangru, Tian Dan, Jing Ke, Xiang Yu and Liu Bang) in the book.

Sima Qian worked hard to collect historical materials, but he did not use all of them. He focused on highlighting the personalities of the characters and the most representative things. Take Lin Xiangru for example. He laid the emphasis on three cases: Returning the Intact Jade to the State of Zhao, the Meeting at Mianchi and Making up with the General. There is another example, when writing about the Prince of Wei, Sima Qian focused on two cases: Inviting Hou Ying and Stealing the Commander's Seal to Save Zhao State. When writing about Tian Dan, he only narrated the story about the "Fire Bull Strategy". For these characters, there should be a lots of things to write about. For example, Tian Dan became the prime minister of the Qi State and saved the prime minister of the Zhao State later. However, Sima Qian did not mention it in the book, because he believed that it was not the title of the prime minister but the "Fire Bull Strategy" that made Tian Dan an immortal figure in the history. He knew that what he wrote about was enough to reflect the personalities and spiritual temperament of the characters. For this purpose, he also adopted the writing skill of "cross reference" to guarantee the completeness of the characters' personalities by mentioning the content that could not be mentioned in the biography of the character in the biography of another character for the reference of the readers. For example, the Prince of Wei had representative political opinions. However, Sima Qian did not mentioned them in the *Biography of the Prince of Wei*, because he believed it was nothing to do with the morality to be courteous to the wise and condescending to scholars that he wanted to highlight in the chapter, but he mentioned them in the *House of Wei* (*Wei Shijia*). That's why many of the characters appeal to the readers. Mao Kun (Ming Dynasty)said, "I wanted to sacrifice my life when reading the biographies of knight-errants, and cry when reading the biographies of Qu Yuan and Jia Sheng, and leave the world when reading the biographies of Lao-Tzu and Lu Zhonglian, and set a great ideal when reading the biography of Li Guang, and bend down to show respect when reading the biography of Shi Jian, and support scholars when reading the biographies of the Lord of Xinling and the Lord of Pingyuan." Today, there are still many controversies on the ways

used by Sima Qian to depict the characters and select the
information for the book. However, to write biographies
is not just to show the information. The personalities of
the characters should be highlighted. In this aspect, Sima
Qian set a good example for the later authors of historical
works. The official histories following the *Records of the
Grand Historian*, such as *The History of the Han Dynasty,
The History of the Later Han Dynasty (Hou Han Shu)*,
the *Romance of the Three Kingdoms (San Guo Zhi)* and
The New History of the Five Dynasties (Xin Wu Dai Shi),
all boast great achievements in depiction of personalities
of characters. However, generally, with the separation of
the historical works and literature in theory, less and less
attention has been paid to the literariness of historical
works. Some authors of historical works even rejected to
show the literariness in their works. The tradition to depict
personalities of characters adopted to write the *Records
of the Grand Historian* was inherited and carried forward
by a number of later authors of single miscellaneous
biographies and biographic proses and novels. The most
outstanding works include the *Postscript of Zhang
Zhongcheng's Biography (Zhang Zhongcheng Zhuan Hou
Xu)* by Han Yu, the *Anecdotes about Taiwei Duan (Duan
Taiwei Yi Shi Zhuang)* by Liu Zongyuan, the *Anecdotes
about Zuo Guangdou (Zuo Zhong Yi Gong Yi Shi)* by
Fang Bao, the *Biography of Liu Yi (Liu Yi Zhuan)* and the
Biography of Qiu Ranke (Qiu Ranke Zhuan), which were

both legends of the Tang Dynasty, and the *Ying Ning*
and *Xiao Xie* in the *Strange Tales of Liaozhai (Liaozhai
Zhi Yi)*. These works show the profound influence of
the *Records of the Grand Historian* on the depiction of
characters in the Chinese literatures.

Fourth, the book indicates strong subjective opinions,
showing what the author liked or hated in an obvious way.
Lu Xun said in his *Outline of the History of Literature of*

Illustration in the *Strange Tales of Liaozhai: Ying Ning*

Han (*Han Wen Xue Shi Gang Yao*) that, "Sima Qian felt so ashamed after he suffered the castration punishment that he exerted all efforts to write the book to tell his story and suffering to the later generations. Although the *Records of the Grand Historian* is in contravention of *The Spring and Autumn Annals* (*Chun Qiu*), it is still a masterpiece of historical works and on a par with the *Lisao*." I wrote in the *Comments on the Annotations of the Records of the Grand Historian* (*Shi Ji Xuan Zhu Ji Shuo*): "It is an anthem of love and a curse of hate, with unutterable sadness and resentment of the author." The reason for this is that Sima Qian was not a politician so that his political opinions could not be directly turned into guiding principles and measures for governance. He was a historian, who could only show his praises and criticisms and his opinions on goodness and evilness through his narration. He put ideal glory on the great, lofty and kind people to show his pursuits for the ideal politics and morality. He rendered the intrinsic hideous side of the contemptible, treacherous and insidious people, showing his furiousness and contempt for these people as well as spurn and castigation on the reactionary force. Guo Moruo wrote in the *Notes on Opinions on Poems* (*Lun Shi Zha Ji*) that, "The spirit of poem lies in its intrinsic rhythm, which is not about the extrinsic rhythm, such as the tones, cadences, strength, length, alliteration and assonance or rhyme, but about the natural emotional change." On this principle, the *Records of the Grand Historian*, with 520,000 Chinese characters, is like a long poem full of sadness and resentment. Moreover, the *Records of the Grand Historian* shows exquisite extrinsic rhythm. For example, the skills of "narrations interspersed with comments", "narrations to take the place of comments", "comments to take the place of narrations" and "combined narrations and comments" were used, making the book a long lyric poetry. Examples for this include the *Biography of Bo Yi*, the *Biography of Qu Yuan* and the *Biographies of Knight-errants*. There are also some chapters with rich lyric and rhythmical contents, such as the *Biography of Lord Pingyuan (Pingyuan Jun Liezhuan)*, the *Biography of Lu Zhonglian* and the *Biography of General Li*. Some chapters include a large amount of quotations from poems, odes and folk songs and proverbs. In addition, the author also designed many singing scenes, such as the *Song of Picking Vetch (Cai Wei Ge)* sung before the death of Bo Yi, the *Song of the Yi River (Yi Shui Ge)*sung before Jing Ke set out for his mission, the *Song of Gaixia (Gaixia Ge)* sung when Xiang Yu was besieged, the Song of Gale (*Da Feng Ge*) sung when Liu Bang returned to his hometown, and the *Song of Honghu (Hong Hu Ge)* when Concubine Qi was crying. All of them enhanced the lyricism of the works. There are also rhymes in some chapters of the book or some parts of a chapter, such as the *Biographies of Jesters (Hua Ji Liezhuan)* and the *Biographies of Soothsayers*. The

Qu Yuan Lonely Recites A Poem drawn by Liang Kai, Song in the Southern Dynasties

rhymes highlight the funny and humorous atmosphere at the same time of enhancing the rhythmicity and lyricism of the writings.

Just because of the consistentintrinsicrhythm and the focus on the expression ways, the *Records of the Grand Historian* shows strong subjectivity, lyricism and imposing sense that were rarely shown by other Chinese proses. Therefore, Liu E, the author of *The Travels of Lao Can (Lao Can You Ji)*, said, "*Lisao* is the cry of Qu Yuan, while the *Records of the Grand Historian* is the cry of Sima Qian." There were only a few of official histories with so strong lyricism and influence, including the *Biography of Su Wu* (Su Wu Zhuan) in *The History of the Han Dynasty* and the *Biographies of the Actors and Actresses* (*Ling Guan Zhuan*) in the *New History of the Five Dynasties*. Most of the later historical works are extremely ordinary and boring. However, many later single miscellaneous biographies inherited and carried forward the strong lyricism of the *Records of the Grand Historian*, such as the *Epitaph for Liu Zongyuan* (*Liu Zihou Mu Zhi Ming*) by Han Yu, the *Biographical Sketch of Deceased Mother* (*Xian Bi Shi Lüe*) by Gui Youguang, and the *Biography of Yan Yingyuan* (*Yan Dianshi Zhuan*) by Shao Changheng. With sadness, loneness or solemnness, they can shock the readers. In this aspect, they are very similar with the *Records of the Grand Historian*.

Fifth, the structure of chapters and the narration and commenting ways adopted for the Records of *the Grand Historian* were imitated by the later authors of biographical literatures and set as models. Zhao Yi (Qing Dynasty) said, "Based on the ancient and contemporary historical materials, Sima Qian took a lead to write general history. The work consists of the annals of the emperors, the genealogies of the noble houses, 10 tables on current events, eight monographs and biographies. Each chapter is ended with *The Grand Historian's Remarks*. It set an

example that followed by many later historians." (*Notes on
22 Histories*) From an overall perspective, it indicated that,
generally, the official histories and many unofficial histories
in the later dynasties imitated the model of the *Records of
the Grand Historian.*

Study on single chapters showed that, each chapter
begins with the introduction to the birthplace of the
leading character, which was followed by the narration of
his (her) life and then his (her) death and the development
of his (her) family after his (her) death. Each chapter
includes the remarks of the author, namely *The Grand
Historian's Remarks.* In most cases, the remarks were
made at the end of the chapter. For some special chapters,
they were put at the beginning. The remarks may be about
the people or the events, the author's feelings, some tales
or supplementary information. Then the book was set as
a criterion for the later official histories and biographies.
The skills used to write the book were even used to write
proses and novels. The *Biography of Mao Ying* (*Mao
Ying Zhuan*) by Han Yu is a funny and humorous prose
containing frustrating feeling and resentment. Its style
and tone are remarkably like that of the *Records of the
Grand Historian.* In addition, quite a number of works
about the legends of the Tang and Song dynasties imitated
the *Records of the Grand Historian.* The only difference is
that the remarks were directly made at the end of a chapter
without any title. The *Strange Tales of Liaozhai* has the

Remarks of the Historian of the Strange(Yi Shi Shi Yue) at the end of each chapter. It is completely an imitation of *The Grand Historian's Remarks* in the *Records of the Grand Historian*.

The longest chapter in the *Records of the Grand Historian* is the *Annals of Qin Shi Huang (Qin Shi Huang Benji)*, with more than 13,000 Chinese characters. The second and third longest chapters are the *Annals of Gaozu (Gaozu Benji)* and the *Annals of Xiang Yu*, respectively with about 10,000 and 6,000 Chinese characters. The shortest one is the *Biography of Sima Rangju*, with only less than 700 Chinese characters. Most of the chapters have 3,000 to 6,000 Chinese characters. They are relatively short compared with many other works. Such arrangement for the sizes of the chapters also has great influence on the later ancient biographical literatures.Among the later official historical works, some are well-known for their length, such as: the *Biography of Wang Mang (Wang Mang Zhuan)* in The *History of the Han Dynasty*, with about 35,000 Chinese characters; the *Annals of Gaozong (Gaozong Benji)* in The *History of the Song Dynasty (Song Shi)*, with about 90,000 Chinese characters; and the *Annals of Shizu (Shizu Benji)* in The *History of the Yuan Dynasty (Yuan Shi)*, with about 180,000 Chinese characters. However, they are exceptions among the ancient classics and should not be classified as literatures. In addition, they are rarely read by people. Most of the ancient biographical literatures and proses and novels are short. There are original biographies, supplementary biographies, tablet inscriptions, epitaphs, allegorical works, miscellaneous proses and "purposed" novels. Each of them has several thousands of Chinese characters.It is the characteristic of the *Records of the Grand Historian* to narrate the stories and depict the characters in a short chapter at the same time of maintaining a high ideological level. It is also one of the fine traditions of the ancient biographical literatures of China.

The *Records of the Grand Historian*, the literature of that time

Chang Sen

Since Lu Xun said that "the *Records of the Grand Historian* is a masterpiece of historical works and on a par with the *Lisao*" (*Outline of the History of Literature of Han, The Complete Works of Lu Xun IX*, People's Literature Publishing House, 1981, P420), the book has been regarded as a rarely great work among the histories and literatures. However, few people mentioned which parts of the book belong to history, which parts belong to literature and which parts are more important.

From the modern academic view, the most obvious feature of the *Records of the Grand Historian* as a historical work is its focus on the living and cultural status of the people in a history of thousands of years. *The Preface of Shi Ji* said that, the *Records of the Grand Historian* contains records from the Yellow Emperor to the Taichu period under the reign of Emperor Wu of Han Dynasty. Zhang Shoujie wrote in his *Correct Interpretation of the Records of the Grand Historian: On Historical Cases* that, "Sima Qian wrote the *Records of the Grand Historian*, which covers a history of 2,413 years from the reigns of the Yellow Emperor, Gaoyang, Gaoxin, Yao and Shun as well as the Xia, Zhou and Qin dynasties to the fourth year of the Tianhan period under the reign of Emperor Wu of Han Dynasty. The book consists of 12 royal annals, 10 tables, eight monographs, 30 genealogies of noble houses and 70 biographies. Each part is indispensable, with systematic narration of the history and the author's praises and admonishments. It sets a good example for later historical works." The academic circle still have some controversies on the events recorded in the book, but no one doubts that the book is unprecedented. This is about the first feature of the *Records of the Grand Historian* as a historical work.

A more profound feature of the *Records of the Grand Historian* as a historical work is its faithfulness to the facts. In accordance with *The History of the Han*

Dynasty: Biography of Sima Qian, many famous scholars, such as Liu Xiang and Yang Xiong, said that "Sima Qian has the talent to write good historical works. He is good at narration, justification without rhetoric, simple and unsophisticated expression without vulgarness as well as direct and faithful record of history without adulation or concealing of evil deeds." Some contemporary scholars said, "The Records of the Grand Historian are faithful records. It is the most excellent work whether in history or in the future, at least in the class society." "Nearly none of the works in the *Twenty-Four Histories* (*Er Shi Si Shi*) is comparable with the *Records of the Grand Historian* in terms of the faithfulness to the facts." (Guo Yuheng, *The History of Chinese Proses I*, Shanghai Chinese Classics Publishing House, 1986, P295 to 296) To be faithful to the historical facts is a very important feature of the *Records of the Grand Historian* as a historical work.

When talking about the expectations for modern science of history, Liang Qichao said, "A good historian is good at organizing the narration of historical facts: horizontally, emphasis should be laid on the backgrounds and interconnections, for example, the relation between event A and event B, to maintain the integrity of the history; vertically, emphasis should be laid on the cause-and-effect relationship between the events, for example, the relationship between the earlier event and the latter event, to maintain the systematicness of the history."

(*Methodology in the Study of Chinese History, Collected Essays from the Ice-Drinker's Studio*, 10th Monographic Series, 73, Zhonghua Book Company, 1989, P34) The *Records of the Grand Historian* shows the historical evolution in a systematic way, namely that it clarifies the relations between the facts. It is the most profound feature of the book as a historical work.

However, from the modern academic perspective, there more profound features of the book than its features as a historical work, namely the features that define the book as a literature. This mainly because:

First, one of the primary goals of Sima Qian to write the *Records of the Grand Historian* is to show his own opinions. He once said, "In the ancient times, many rich and noble people did not leave their names in the history. Only these extremely outstanding and extraordinary people can be well-known to the later generations. (Such as) Ji Chang made supplement to the *Book of Changes* (*Zhou Yi*) when he was prisoned; Confucius wrote *The Spring and Autumn Annals* when he was suffering difficulties; Qu Yuan wrote the *Lisao* when he was exiled; Zuo Qiuming wrote *The Discourses of the States* after he lost his sight; Sun Bin wrote the *Strategies for Wars* after his knee caps were removed; Lyu Buwei wrote the *Mister Lyu's Spring and Autumn Annals* (*Lyu Shi Chun Qiu*) after he was relegated to Shu; Han Fei wrote 300 articles, such as *On Difficulties* (*Shuo Nan*), *Lonely Indignation* (*Gu Fen*) and *Poems*

(*Shi*), when was kept in captivity in the Qin State. They tried to express their repression, depression, confusion as well as ideals and ambitions through the narration of the historical events. For example, Zuo Qiuming who lost his sight and Sun Bin who could never stand up again knew that they would never get the chance to hold an important post. Therefore, they wrote the works to show their discontent and indignation and their thoughts." (*A Letter to Ren An*) Here we will not discuss about whether the opinions of Sima Qian on these classics and the reasons why they were written are right or not. It should be noticed that, the words of the author explained his intention to follow the steps of the ancient sages to show his feelings and opinions. In addition, the author also had a so-called "selfish motive". He said that he dragged out an ignoble existence after being castrated just because the *Records of the Grand Historian* had not been finished. In *A Letter to Ren An*, he mentioned, "I do not want to die because of my 'selfish motive'." The goal or the "selfish motive" is just the reason why the book includes so strong personal opinions of the author and is even regarded as an "excellent biography" of the author (Li Chang Zhi, *Style and Personalities of Sima Qian*, SDX Joint Publishing Company, 1984, P220), or why it "reflects the whole spiritual world of the author" (Nie Shiqiao, *The Essays on Sima Qian*, Beijing Normal University Publishing Group, 1987, P43). However, most parts of the *Records of the*

Photocopy of *The Summary of Arts*

Grand Historian did not directly show the opinions of
the author. As Liu Xizai said, "The essential of the work
of Sima Qian is to make everything the carrier to show
the feelings of the author even without direct mention of
his opinions." (*The Summary of Arts • The Summary of
Literature*)

Second, Sima Qian pursued literary grace when
writing the *Records of the Grand Historian*. He expressed
his feelings after being castrated: "I am so timid that I still
want to live. However, I also know the difference between
such survival and death. How can I just wallow in the
grief of the prison life and humiliation! Even the slaves
and maidservants may kill themselves when suffering
insults, let alone me, who was in such a helpless situation.

The season for me to endure the humiliation to survive is that I still wish to finish the book. If I died without any accomplishments, the book would never get the chance to exist in the future. (*A Letter to Ren An*)

In fact, both the opinions and the literary grace shown by the book present the emotional and rhetorical styles of Sima Qian. From the modern academic perspective, they are literatures rather than histories. German scholar Ernst Cassirer wrote, "The personal style which we feel in every line of a great historian is not an emotional or rhetorical style. A rhetorical style may have many merits; it may move and delight the reader. But it misses the principal point: it cannot lead us to an intuition and to a free and unbiased judgment of things and events."(*An Essay on Man*, Shanghai Translation Publishing House, 1985, P241 to 242) Literary historian Qian Jibo said, "Histories should tell the true history. To a historian, it is important to record the history in a faithful way rather than expressing emotions; then he will be able to make adiaphorous judgement of the events and people." (*The History of Chinese Literature I*, Zhonghua Book Company, 1993, P5)

Third, the *Records of the Grand Historian* highly focuses on the personalities of the characters. Liang Qichao said that the first key point of the *Records of the Grand Historian* is the "focus on people... The book consists of 130 chapters. Except for the 10 tables and eight monographies, the rest chapters are all biographies.

There were no such structure in the foreign historical books or the ancient Chinese books before the *Records of the Grand Historian*. It should be a shortage to structure a historical work with so many biographies of individuals. As a result, the book shows the history of the people but not the society. This is a shortage. However, it is a merit of the book to tell the detailed stories of the people who initiated the social changes for the reference of the later generations...Most of the later histories feature biographies based on history, while the *Records of the Grand Historian* features depiction of people based on history." (*Interpretations of the Classics and Ways of Reading, Collected Essays from the Ice-Drinker's Studio, 9th Monographic Series*, 72, P19 to 20). Essentially, the "people" usually play a core role in the modern science of history, which, however, focuses more on the generality of the people than the individual personalities. Therefore, the modern science of history is about the people but does not highlight specific individual figures. However, the depiction of individual figures is the biggest highlight of the *Records of the Grand Historian* when it is deemed as a literature.

Anyway, it is hard to define the nature of the book based on the modern subject classification. We can only know which parts of the book belong to history, which parts belong to literature and which features are more important. However, it is still not enough. What's more important, the book contains a great number of elements beyond the boundaries of modern literature and history, and it is hard to classify these elements. From the traditional academic perspective, these elements correspond to the essence of the Confucian classics. The Confucian classics composed the traditional academic system with the most Chinese characteristics. They held the orthodox academic position after Emperor Wu of Han Dynasty ordered to ban from hundred schools of thoughts to venerate Confucianism. However, their origin can be traced back to the Spring and Autumn and Warring States Periods, when a number of important Confucians created a variety of books. The Confucian classics mainly include the *Book of Changes*, *The Book of Documents*, *The Book of Songs*, *The Book of Rites* and *The Spring and Autumn Annals*. Some scholars engaged in study of the Confucian classics believe that these classics bear the special values of the Confucian school so that they interpret them by laying emphasis on carrying forward the concepts of rites, kindheartedness, the five major virtues or principle of feudal moral conducts and try hard to put them into practice to standardize the behaviors of the social members, the relationship among them and the order of social groups. The literary historians usually neglect the fact that one of the primary goals of Sima Qian to write the *Records of the Grand Historian* was to carry forward the concepts embraced by the Confucian classics and praise individual behaviors, relationships and social order in line with the values adopted in the Confucian classics.

In accordance with *The Preface of Shi Ji*, Sima Tan, who was Sima Qian's father, made the determination to write a historical work, aiming to inherit the spirit of the former sages to amend the *Commentaries on the Book of Changes (Yi Zhuan)*, make supplement to *The Spring and Autumn Annals* and explore the original meanings of *The Book of Songs*, *The Book of Documents*,*The Book of Rites* and *The Book of Music (Yue Jing)*. Knowing that he could not finish it, he told his son to continue the writing. Sima Qian promised, "Dare I to refuse it?"Modestly, Sima Qian said, "(The book) just tells stories and record history. It cannot be compared with *The Spring and Autumn Annals*." In his opinion,*The Spring and Autumn Annals* is not an ordinary historical work, but a classic that put the wrong to the right. So, he wrote in the preface that, "*The Spring and Autumn Annals* tells the political principles of Yu of Xia, Tang of Shang and King Wen of Zhou; it distinguishes the guiding principles for dealing with others, makes things that were confusing and difficult to understand clear, defines the boundaries of the right and wrong, enables the indecisive people to make up their mind, glorifies the virtues and censures vices, pays respect to the sages and belittles the unworthy. It keeps the records of the conquered states and continues the genealogies. It promotes the remedy to political defects and the emerging of the obsolescent undertakings. Those are important points for governance." Related to this, The Book of Songs, *The Book of Documents*, *The Book of Rites* and *The Book of Music* should also be paid enough attention, because Sima Qian believed that these classics bear the values and concepts of the Confucian school and have important functions on politics, education and ethics. Actually, the purpose of Sima Qian to write the book was to carry forward the values and concepts contained in the Confucian classics and realize the goals for which these classics were written. To a large extent, the *Records of the Grand Historian* focuses more on the Confucian classics.

In the preface, Sima Qian revealed the reasons for writing these chapters under the book, which can be used as the key basis for the interpretation of the book. For example, "To praise the morality and righteousness of King Zhuang of Chu, the *House of Chu* (*Chu Shijia*) was wrote...To praise Goujian for cultivating morality in the land of the barbarians and defeating the powerful Wu State and showing loyalty and respect to the Zhou Dynasty, the *House of King Goujian of Yue* was written...To praise Lord Li of Zheng for helping King Hui, the *House of Zheng* (*Zheng Shijia*) was written...To praise Zhao Yang for putting down the turbulence of the royal family of Zhou, the *House of Zhao* (*Zhao Shijia*) was written... To praise Han Jue for his assistance for the Jin State, the *House of Han* (*Han Shijia*) was written...To praise the

Chen Duxiu

King Wei of Qi and King Xuan of Qi for supporting the Zhou Dynasty, the *House of Tian Jingzhong (Tian Wan) (Tian Jingzhong Wan Shijia)* was written... The Zhou Dynasty is declining and the dukes and princes are unscrupulous. Confucius felt sad about the dilapidation of the rite and music systems and then devoted himself to making academic study, aiming to rebuild benevolent government and rectify the social order. He left the Six Classics (Liu Yi) to the later generations. So the *House of Confucius (Kong Zi Shijia)* was written...When others were contending for power and profit, Bo Yi and Shu Qi showed great kindheartedness and righteousness. They even starved themselves to death to resign the sovereign authority. Their morality was praised by the world people. So, the *Biography of Bo Yi* was written." This shows that it is a basic purpose of the *Records of the Grand Historian* to praise the Confucian values and conduct standards (such as morality and righteousness) and the individual behaviors, relationships and social order that meet the Confucian values and conduct standards(such as being righteous, cultivating morality, putting down turbulence, making academic study, adopting benevolent governance, rectifying social order, respecting the emperor and restricting the power of the dukes and princes).

Such feature of the *Records of the Grand Historian* is not contradictory with the concepts embraced by the classical literature represented by the Confucian classics, but is incompatible with the modern literary concepts. Chen Duxiu, who was one of the leaders of the May 4 New Culture Movement, said, "Literature is not a moral carrier." (*On Literary Revolution, The Articles of Chen Duxiu*, 1987, P96-97) In the early period of the 20th century, literary historian Zheng Binyu said, "The essence of literature is the emotions beyond realistic pursuit for material gains. It is the most sentimental parts in the heart of people and the most moving narration instead of the knowledge about the truth or the sermons about kindness." (*The History of the Changes of the Chinese Literature*, Volume 3, Qian Lun, Zhongzhou Ancient Books Publishing House, 1991, P6-7) However, the elements concerning the Confucian classics in the *Records of the Grand Historian* are just the moral carriers and the sermons about kindness.

The modern histories also reject the elements concerning the Confucian classics. Liang Qichao said, "The nature of historical works is different from other kinds of academic works; I dare not to say whether some people are capable of writing objective histories. However, all these people who want to become historians encourage themselves with the principle to tell the truth, namely being perspicacious and unbiased and faithful to the historical facts, whether when collecting the historical materials or making narrations and comments, to maintain the authenticity of the history. So, I think that the later historians should, as much as possible, restrict the subjectivity and be loyal to the objective facts and adhere to the goal to tell the true history. In this way, we can have trustable and good historical works." (*Methodology in the Study of Chinese History, Collected Essays from the Ice-Drinker's Studio*, 10th Monographic Series, 73, P32-33) The *Records of the Grand Historian* was well-known as a good historical work in the ancient times, but it is not an objective one. Liang Qichao said, "For politicians, the later generations will have evaluation on what they did, whether their merits or demerits. However, the historians should not make evaluation. Instead, they just need to specifically record the experiences of the politicians and the facilities. That is the responsibility of the historians." (*Methodology in the Study of Chinese History [Supplement], Collected Essays from the Ice-Drinker's Studio*, 12th Monographic Series, 99, P73) He said, "The right way to write history, no matter what kind of history, is to tell the truth without criticisms and comments; otherwise, it is should be a second-rate work. For example, for a biography, the most talented historian should be able to tell the truth about the person without judgement but enable the readers to see the position or value of the person through his narration." (The same as above, P80) However, Sima Qian was obviously an exception. As he said in The *Preface of Shi Ji*, he set many people and events as models for moral qualities and social achievements. In that case, how could the work be written without judgements and criticisms? Sima Qian believed that the purpose of Confucius to write *The Spring and Autumn Annals* was to "dispel the suspicions, identify what is the right or wrong, avoid hesitation, praise the good deeds and criticize the evil deeds, and show respect to the sages and scorn the unworthy". Therefore, with the goal to carry forward the spirit embraced by *The Spring and Autumn Annals*, Sima Qian wrote the *Records of the Grand Historian* with the spirit of criticism. Liang Qichao said, "Based on the latest historical viewpoints, the historical works focusing on people have many defects. They are more like the tools used to praise some people. Many people believe that it's the biggest shortcoming of the Chinese historical works. To a large extent, we should

Portrait of Confucius

admit that it is the truth, because the historical works laying too much emphasis on the people incline to exhibit virtues and expose vices so that they almost look like a textbook on morality cultivation and even lose the essential features as historical works." (The same with above, P29) "We may carry forward what we believe in any ways except for relying on the historical works. It is unhelpful but harmful." (The same with above, P15) The *Records of the Grand Historian*, which bases on the Confucian values to evaluate the behaviors and relationships of the social members and the social order and praise the deeds of being righteous, cultivating morality, putting down turbulence, making academic study, adopting benevolent governance and rectifying social order, obviously goes against the modern academic positioning on the science of history.

Therefore, in the modern sense, the *Records of the Grand Historian* is neither completely a historical work nor a literary work. Many elements in the book are beyond all the modern academic categories and highlight the essences of the Confucian classics. "Literature" appeared at the end of the Spring and Autumn period. It is a historical fact that, before the Wei and Jin dynasties, the *Records of the Grand Historian* was deemed as a "literature".*The Analects of Confucius: Xian Jin*, which tells that everybody has his strong points, said "Distinguished for their virtuous principles and practice, there were Yan Yuan, Min Ziqian, Ran Boniu, and Zhong Gong; for their ability in speech,

Zai Wo and Zi Gong; for their talents in politics, Ran You and Ji Lu; for their literary achievements, Zi You and Zi Xia." Based on the existing materials, it should be the first time that the concept of literature was put forward. To the Warring States period, even all the written works were deemed as "literatures". For example, Mo Tzu mentioned "literary creation" and "conversation" in the same breath (See *Mo Tzu: Anti-Fatalism [II]*, *Mo Zi : Fei Ming Zhong*, etc.) "Literature" refers to "all the knowledge written by people." (Shi Changdong, *Comments on Aesthetic Ideology of Scholars in the Pre-Qin Period*, Zhonghua Book Company, 1979, P41). At the end of the Warring States period, Hsun Tsu showed his view on "literature", which was an inheritance of the Confucian concept and laid the focus on the six classics. "Even the descendants of the ordinary people, as long as they can learn literature well and behave righteously, they can be high-ranking officials." (*Hsun Tsu: Governance, Xun Zi : Wang Zhi*) Han Fei, who was the student of Hsun Tsu would like to refer the literatures and classics of all the other academic schools except for the legalist school. He wrote: "It was different in the turbulent times. The ordinary people struggled against the orders of the state leader with their academic standpoints, and violated the laws by their private behaviors. Therefore, the state leader gave up the legal ways to respect and relies heavily on the scholars' wisdom and behaviors. That's why so many people engaged in academic activities in the world." (*Han Fei Zi: Wen Bian*) He also wrote: "People who wanted to become immortals relying on necromancies were offenders. However, they were called learned scholars by the world people." (*Han Fei Zi: Liu Fan*) His opinions indicated that "literature" had become a term that was familiar to the society. In the Han Dynasty, "literature" was defined to cover all the classics represented by the Confucian classics. Wang Chong said, "The scholars shall create works based on the five classics and six arts, the works of different academic schools, the treatises, the memorials to the throne and the literary virtue." (*Lun Heng: Yi Wen*)In the Han Dynasty, the schools in the princedoms taught the "princedom literature", which was actually the Confucian classics. To sum up, the "literature" at that time had more multiple and complicated meanings. In addition, there were no other concepts, such as the concept of "science of history", coexisting at the same time. It is the origin of the Chinese literature developed in the following more than 2,000 years.

At that time, the *Records of the Grand Historian* was completely deemed as a literary work. Therefore, to faithfully and completely restore the history, the literary historians have to first faithfully and completely restore the "literature". However, since the 20th century, what the literary historians have been doing is to safeguard parts of the fragments of that part of history with the modern "literary" concepts. Then, on what basis can they say that they are interpreting the "literary" history?

The ingenuity of Sima Qian in selecting historical materials

Tian Jujian

Since the ancient time, the *Records of the Grand Historian* by Sima Qian has been read by numerous people, from scholars engaged in historical studies to ordinary people, and from the aged to the young. It has the charm to attract you to continue to read as long as you open it. There are many reasons for that, but one of the main reasons is that Sima Qian was so good at selecting historical materials, especially "collecting the lost works and ancient materials" (*The Preface of Shi Ji*) and "selecting the elegant works." (*Annals of the Five Emperors*) He aimed to select the most typical historical materials based on a sufficient preliminary collection to support the conception and structuring of the book and highlight the inherent characteristics and features of the characters.

Jian Bozan had comments on the ingenuity and ability of Sima Qian in selecting historical materials. In his work titled *On Sima Qian's History*, he wrote: "For two thousands of years, there is no people who read the *Records of the Grand Historian* without praise. Sima Qian's narrations are really vivid, serious but literarily graceful. It is not the style of writing but his ingenuity in organization of historical materials that makes the work a masterpiece. For example, to write the biography of Bo Yi, he included the *Song of Western Mountain* (*Xi Shan Zhi Ge*) to manifest the moral courage of Bo Yi; when writing the biographies of Confucius and Mencius, he quoted their words to show their opinions; when writing the biographies of Lao-Tzu and Chuang-Tzu, he included their works to clarify their academic standpoints; when writing the biographies of Qu Yuan and Jia Sheng, he included their poems to highlight their achievements in literature; when writing about scholar, he mentioned their inheritance from their teachers to explain the origin; when writing the biographies of Guan Zhong and Yan Ying, he included their political achievements to show their contributions in governance; when writing the biographies of Tian Dan and Yue Yi, he included the wars they attended to show their military contributions; when writing the biographies of Zhang Yi and Su Qin, he included their political lobbying experiences to praise their abilities in lobbying; when writing the biographies of usurers, he included their properties to show their richness; when writing the biographies of the assassins, he highlighted their braveness toward death to manifest their devotion; when writing the biographies of the knight-errants, he focused on their morality to keep promise to highlight their chivalrous spirit; when writing the biographies of the jesters, he included the jokes for sarcastic effect; when writing the biographies of flatterers, he included their behaviors to basely offer to serve the bigwig to show their impudence. To sum up, Sima Qian captured and expounded the characteristics of every character to make them vividly revealed on the paper." (*Selected Papers of Jian Bozan on the Science of History II*, People's Publishing House, 1990, P117)

I deeply agree with Jian's conclusions and examples mentioned above, which suddenly enlightened me. Here I add some examples drawn from the *Records of the Grand Historian* as supplement.

The *Biographies of Sun Tzu and Wu Qi* are about two well-known strategists. The story of Sun Wu (Sun Tzu) is very typical. In regular mode, the biography for

Sword of King Helu of Wu State

Sun Wu may center on *The Art of War by Sun Tzu* (*Sun Zi Bing Fa*), which is the most representative work of the military strategist in the Spring and Autumn period. However, Sima Qian selected the materials that seemed far away from the main theme. He laid the emphasis on the case that Sun Wu maneuvered his tactical deployment of troops with the maids in the palace instead of the soldiers. The story is like this: "Helu (the King of Wu) asked, 'Can you maneuver with the maids?' Sun Wu asked, 'Yes, I can.' Then, the king called together 100 maids. Sun Wu divided them into two teams headed by two favorite concubines of the king. Every lady held a halberd. Then Sun Wu ordered, 'Do you know where your heart, left hand, right hand and back are?' The ladies said, 'Yes'. Sun Wu said, 'When I said *forward*, you should look at the direction that you heart faces; when I said *left*, you should look at the direction at your left hand; When I said right, you should look at the direction at your right side; when I said *back*, you should look at the direction at you back.' The ladies answered, 'Yes'. Then, Sun Wu ordered people to put the axes and other implements of punishment in order and then repeated the orders for several times. After that, he beat the drum and issued an order. When he said *right*, the ladies laughed without response to the order. Sun Wu said, 'They are not familiar with the orders, and this should be the mistake of the commander.' So, he repeated the orders and then asked them to turn right. The ladies laughed again. Sun Wu said, 'They do not know the disciplines and are still unfamiliar with the orders, and this should be the mistake of the commander.' Then, he repeated the disciplines and orders and asked them to turn left. The ladies laughed again. Sun Wu said, 'That they did not know the disciplines and were unfamiliar with the orders should be the mistake of the commander. However, everything has been clearly told. In that case, they still failed to act in accordance with the order, and this should be the mistake of the military officers and the soldiers.' Therefore, he ordered to kill the heads of the two teams. The king who was watching it was surprised when Sun Wu ordered to kill his two favorite concubines so that he said to Sun Wu, 'Now I know you are very good at military practices. I cannot lose the two concubines; otherwise, I will feel that food is tasteless. Please do not kill them.' Sun Wu answered, 'I have accepted the order to be the general, who has the right to not accept the order of the king when doing military affairs.' So, the two concubines were killed and two new heads of the teams were appointed. Then, Sun Wu beat the drum and issued orders again. The ladies dared not to ignore the orders and disciplines any more. Therefore, Sun Wu sent an officer to report to the king, 'The teams are ready, and your majesty may use them in any way, even letting them go to extremely dangerous areas.'The king answered, 'Tell the general to stop the maneuver and go back to the guesthouse to have a rest. I will not go downstairs to watch it.' Sun Wu sighed and said, 'It seems that the king just appreciates my military theories but does not want me to practice it.' Since then, the king knew that Sun Wu was good at military practices and appointed him the general." The story showed the wisdom, courage and military talent of Sun Wu. As to the military strategies and contributions of Sun Wu, the author just use two sentences to summarize. The first one is at the beginning, as the King of Wu said, "I have read all your 13 articles." The second one is at the end of the chapter: "Later, the Wu State defeated the Chu State on the west and occupied Yingdu, and overawed the Qi State and Jin State on the north, winning a high prestige among the states. For this, Sun Wu made great contributions!"

The *Biography of Zhang Yi (Zhang Yi Liezhuan)* is about the activities of the political strategists in the Warring States period. The political strategists, who usually lived in the turbulent times and devoted themselves to realizing universal peace and order, promoted their political view with a glib tongue and had no regard for their own lives and reputation. Zhang Yi, who embraced the "horizontal strategy" (alliance with the great power of Qin), once traveled southward, trying to persuade the Chu State to accept the strategy. The steward of the Prime Minister's Mansion fabricated a charge against him for stealing jade and lashed and expelled him. The injured Zhang Yi was teased by his wife, who said, "Alas! How could you be treated like this if you had not tried to persuade them?" Zhang Yi did not answer the question but said, "Look at me. Is my tongue still there?" His wife laughed and said, "Yes, it is there." Zhang Yi said, "Then, it is enough." The simple and humorous dialogue between the husband and his wife exactly depicts the characteristics of Zhang Yi's job and the vivid images of the characters. Such typical materials make the political strategist especially glamorous. If they were used to depict people engaged in other sectors, it may be ludicrous and ridiculous.

The *Biography of Li Si* (*Li Si Liezhuan*) is about the tortuous and miserable life of Li Si, who did not have any ambition but was very greedy for wealth and honor. Born as an ordinary person, young Li Si once worked as a low-level official at a county government. "One day, he saw a mouse eating dirty things in the toilet near his office. Every time when people or dogs came, it felt frightened and escaped soon. Later, Li Si saw a mouse eating corns in the granary, without fear of any people or dogs. Then

Li Si sighed and said, 'It is the same way to the people. How you will be treated depends on where you lived.'" The shortsighted Li Si knew the difference between the people of different classes from the example of the mice and then set his life goal to "have enough food to eat and live in a big house without fear of any others". To get out of the lowly and poor environment, Li Si began to make great efforts to learn the ways of governance from Hsun Tsu. Laster, he assisted the First Emperor of Qin to unify the country and held the position as the prime minister. After the emperor died, Huhai, son of the emperor, plotted with eunuch Zhao Gao to kill the original successor Fusu and usurp the throne. Li Si agreed to help them. However, after Huhai and Zhao Gao achieved their goals, they made a false countercharge against Li Si for attempting to establish his own kingdom and sentenced him to death by cutting him in two at the waist. The typical historical materials mentioned above serve as a main line throughout the process, just like an outline that enables the reader to have a general understanding of the whole work.

The *Biographies of Assassins* is about a number of people with lofty ideals, who inspired awe by upholding justice and facing death unflinchingly. Fan Yuqi is one of the most outstanding ones among them. In the Warring State period, Crown Prince Dan worried that the Yan State would be completely annihilated by the Qin State. So, he asked Jing Ke to assassinate the king of the Qin State. Jing

Portrait of Xiao He,
Chancellor of Han Dynasty

Ke said that, only with gifts of the head of General Fan
Wuqi and the map of Dukang could he won the trust of
the king of the Qin State before killing him. Dan felt it was
too cruel to treat Fan in that way. So, Jing Ke found Fan
and said, "The Qin State killed your parents and relatives.
They even offered a reward of 1,000-jin gold and official
title for the person who can cut you head. What can you do
with it?" Fan sighed and cried, "Whenever I thought about
it, I felt so sad, but I have no idea about what to do."Jing
Ke said, "I know the measure to eliminate the risk for the
Yan State and revenge for you. Do you want to know?" Fan
asked, "What is it?" Jing Ke said, "I have to kill you and

give your head to the king of the Qin State. Then, when the king meets with me, and I will get the chance to grasp his sleeve with my left hand and kill him with dagger. In this way, I can revenge for you and sweep away the insult suffered by the Yan State. What do you think about it?" Fan took off his sleeve and walked closely to Jing Ke and said, "I lived with the hate day and night. You just taught me the way today." Then, he killed himself. The story reflects the strong character of the assassins. The author applied the historical materials in an exactly proper way. Only the assassins like Fan Yuqi could do things like that.

The *House of Chancellor Xiao (Xiao Xiang Guo Shijia)* shows the typical way adopted by the author to use the historical materials. It is about Xiao He, who was recognized and appointed chancellor by Liu Bang, namely the first emperor of the Han Dynasty. After unifying the country, Liu Bang appointed the officials according to their contributions. He gave the first-class reward to Xiao He. This aroused intensive objection of the military officials, who said, "We fought hard with the enemies in tens of or even more than one hundred battles, and occupied numerous cities of different sizes. What did Xiao He do? He did not make any contributions except for writing and discussion. Why he was rewarded like this?" The emperor said, "Do you know hunting?" The military officials said, "Yes." "Do you know hunting by dogs?" They asked, "Yes." Then the emperor said, "When hunting, the dogs capture and kill the preys, while the people are in charge of find the preys and give the commands to the dogs. Your contributions are like that of the dogs, while Xiao He's are like that of the people." The reason for Liu Bang to prevail over the dissenting views was that he saw the extraordinary talent of Xiao He in governance. It said, "After Liu Bang's army entered Xianyang, while the military generals and soldiers were busy in taking the money and properties, only Xiao He found the books and documents and preserved them. So, after Liu Bang became the emperor, he appointed Xiao He as the chancellor." This story makes the finishing point and highlights the typical character of Xiao He under the typical environment, showing the inevitability for Xiao He to be appointed the first chancellor of the Western Han Dynasty.

There are a lot of such examples in the *Records of the Grand Historian*. Sima Qian has great talent in selecting materials to make the articles more convincing and emotionally appeal. That's why many parts of the book became classics that were passed down from one generation to another and some stories were even made idioms, for example, "calling a stag a horse" ("calling white black") in the *Annals of Qin Shi Huang*, "acting with a hidden motive", "breaking the caldrons and sinking the boats" (cutting off all means of retreat), and "being besieged on all sides" in the *Annals of Xiang Yu*, "planning and preparing for an uprising" in the *House of Chen She (Chen*

She Shi Jia), "*The young man is promising and worthy to be taught*" in the *House of Marquis of Liu*, "relieving the besieged by besieging the base of the besiegers" in the *Biographies of Sun Tzu and Wu Qi*, "offering a humble apology" in the *Biographies of Lian Po and Lin Xiangru*, "Changing the flag to take over" in the *Biography of the Marquis of Huaiyin*, "volunteering one's services" in the *Biography of Lord Pingyuan*, and "crowing like a cock and snatching like a dog" (small tricks) in the *Biography of Lord Mengchang (Mengchang Jun Liezhuan)*.

To sum up, it is an effective way to avoid monotonous writing by properly selecting historical materials, especially selecting typical materials.

Chinese constellations in the work of Sima Qian

Du Shengyun

At the clear night, the shining stars are like numerous gems in black velvet, running in some way. They have attracted the attention of the human beings since the ancient times. After many years, the human beings began to know the stars. Then, they used them to identify direction and seasons and then to tell fortune. These functions of astrology make the stars more solemn, majestic and mysterious in people's mind. The ancient Chinese call the fixed stars or the patterns formed up by several or more fixed stars "Chinese constellations".

Sima Qian mentioned the "Chinese constellations" that had been recognized by people by that time in the chapter of *Astronomy* (*Tian Guan Shu*), leaving valuable scientific documents for the later generations and doing a pioneer job to include astronomy in a historical book.

Why did he do so? Sima Qian said, "Since there were people, is there any state leader who did not make the calendar according to the running of the sun, moon and stars?" The *Astronomy* said that, since entering the clan society, the leader of the clans had been telling the people the time by observing the running of the sun, moon and stars (also see the *Calendars, Li Shu*). The inheritance and development of the tradition just indicate that the kings or emperors of all the dynasties deemed making and issuing calendars as a symbol of imperial power. Calendars were made based on observation of the movements of the sun and the moon. The more knowledge about the fixed stars the people acquired, the more accurate the research on the movements of the sun, the moon and the five major planets would be. This was related to politics. Therefore, it is not strange that the Chinese constellations were mentioned in the historical work.

Fixed star observation started every early in the ancient China. A number of classics in the pre-Qin period, including *The Book of Songs*, *The Book of Documents* and the *Book of Changes*, include relevant records, reflecting the knowledge of fixed stars of the people in these periods. Take *The Book of Songs* for example. Many songs mention the Chinese constellations. For example, in the *Southern Shao: Little Stars* (*Shao Nan: Xiao Xing*): "Little Stars are twinkling. Star-clusters are winkling."It is about the *Can Constellation* and the *Mao Constellation*. In the *Songs of Tang: Bundled Firewood* (*Tang Feng: Chou Mou*): "Like dried hay bundled in wedding ties, I see the *Can Constellation* in the eastern skies." Here the *Can Constellation* refers to the Orion. In The *Mountain Gale and Other Odes: The Far East* (*Gu Feng Zhi Shi: Da Dong*): "The Winnow Star in the southern sky, cannot winnow any rye. The Ladle Star in the north ashine, cannot ladle any wine." It is about the *Qi Constellation* and *Dou Constellation*. It is widely known that "In July the Fire Star is hardly spotted; in September winter coats are allotted." It originated from the *Songs of Bin: July*. Here the Fire Star is about the Antares. The *Book of Songs* also mentioned other Chinese constellations. Statistics show that about 50 fixed stars are mentioned in the early works of the ancient China.

Many works written in the Spring and Autumn and the Warring States periods include records of the Chinese constellations, such as *The Spring and Autumn Annals, The Discourses of the States, Er Ya, Proceedings of Government in the Different Months* (*Yue Ling*), *The*

Songs of Chu (*Chu Ci*) and The Book of Rites. More than 140 stars that had not been mentioned before these works appeared. In addition, before the Han Dynasty, there had been various works on astrology, which had a lot of records of the Chinese constellations. For example, the Shi Shen of the Wei States wrote the *Tian Wen* (with eight volumes). Unfortunately, the original book has been lost. However, there are many quotations in other works, reflecting that the book should include a great number of records of the Chinese constellations. To sum up, the people before Sima Qian had known more than 500 fixed stars.

Sima Qian was born in the family with many ancestors working as official historians. At that time, the historians should be proficient in astronomy. Therefore, Sima Qian was very diligent in learning astronomy when he was young. After holding the position as the *Taishiling*, he got the chance to read more documents and materials. All of those mentioned above created good conditions for Sima Qian to make a summary of the Chinese constellations that had been identified before the Han Dynasty. In the chapter of *Astronomy*, he recorded 558 stars and created an extremely vivid and unique system of Chinese constellations, laying a foundation for the naming of the Chinese constellations.

The unique system of Chinese constellations shows the ingenious star identification methods created by Sima

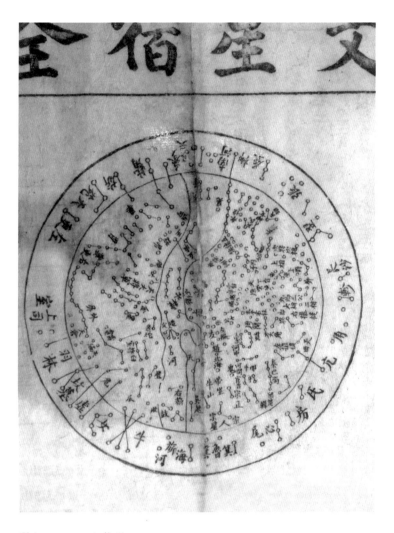

Chinese constellation map

Qian. It indicates the calculation methods concerning the Jupiter cycle and the movements of the sun, the moon and the five major stars, the knowledge and naming of special astronomical phenomena in the ancient China as well as the astronomical phenomena and changes recorded by Sima Qian based on his own observation. It makes the *Records of the Grand Historian* a rare historical work with knowledge on astronomy in the world.

Many people believe that the inclusion of the Chinese constellations in a historical work will make the book boring. However, with extraordinary wisdom, rich imagination and excellent writing skills, Sima Qian made the chapter of *Astronomy* very interesting.

Before Sima Qian, the system of the Chinese constellations had taken initial shape. It consisted of four images (representing four directions) and the 28 constellations. The four images included Black Dragon, Vermilion Bird, White Tiger and Tortoise, which represented the star images seen in spring from the eastern, southern, western and northern sides. Each image was divided into seven *She*. Generally, the moon passes by one *She* each day. Therefore, there were totally 28 *She*, which were called 28 constellations. At the latest, an integrated system had been established by the Spring and Autumn period. Then, Sima Qian improved it into one with five "palaces" and 28 constellations. Compared with the earlier system, the constellation system of Sima Qian had the following major characteristics: 1. five "palaces" representing the star images at five directions, especially the newly added "central palace"; 2. unified naming of the constellations; 3. mentioning of star identification methods, records of relative positions of constellations and description of appearances of constellations; 4. strong literary flavor and vivid description. There is a brief introduction to the constellations mentioned in the chapter of *Astronomy*, showing the ingenuity of Sima Qian in the creation of the work.

The vast galaxy

The "central palace" with the Polaris (*Taiyi* in Chinese) in the center covered the circumpolar zone where the Big Dipper sat. As Sima Qian described, it was the "political center" in the sky. He wrote: "Taiyi permanently sits here", indicating that the Polaris surrounded by other stars nearly doesn't move, as grounds for regarding its supreme position in the sky. It was described like this: "The three stars near Taiyi are like three ministers, while four hook-like stars at its back are like the concubines and the 12 peripheral stars are like vassals."

In addition, the Big Dipper in Sima Qian's telling also reflected the supreme authority of the "central palace". In *The Book of Songs*, dipper was compared to tool used to ladle out wine. However, in Sima Qian's work, it was compared to the carriage for the emperor, with higher position. It "sits in the center and controls the surrounding environment", and "plays an important role in determining time, seasons, directions and positions". In fact, the description in Sima Qian's work has scientific basis. The Big Dipper is indeed an indicator for direction. Sitting opposite to the Polaris, it helps the people find the true north. In addition, it can be used to determine seasons. The *Heguanzi* (Han Dynasty) said that, "When the dipper arm points east, it is in spring; when it points south, it is in summer; when it points west, it is in autumn; when it points north, it is in winter." It indicated that the ancient Chinese used to divide the seasons based on the direction of the arm of the Big Dipper.

Sima Qian shared his experience in star identification with simple descriptions. He used the Big Dipper as a key to star identification: "Along the extending line of the dipper arm, we will find a shining star, which is the Arcturus. Along the extending line of the Polestar and Mizar, we will find the Spica. Along the southward extension of the link between the two stars before and behind the Alioth, we will find the South Dipper, which looks like a dipper formed up by six stars. By linking the first four stars of the Big Dipper two by two and then extending toward the opposite direction of the arm of the dipper, we will find the head of the *Can Constellation*." It is so smart a summarization, which can help people find the South Dipper or the *Can Constellation* based on the Big Dipper.

Sima Qian unified the "eastern palace" with the "central palace" in a perfect way. He wrote: "The *Xin Constellation* is the hall for the emperor of the sky to issue orders. The bigger star represents the emperor, while the two smaller ones represent the princes. The three stars should not stand in a direct line, it is inappropriate." Here, the *Xin Constellation* is compared to the emperor's hall for issuing orders to subtly corresponding to the image of the Black Dragon in the earlier system of Chinese constellations and establish connections with the "central palace". The descriptions about the three stars make it easy for people to identify these stars and become interested in them. Although the saying that the wording that the three stars should not stand in a direct line is full of wit and humor, deeply impressing. In summer, the three stars show in the southern sky, with the central one in red color and especially shining, which is just the Fire Star mentioned in the *Songs of Bin: July*.

The Arcturus at the "horn" of the "dragon" was compared by Sima Qian to the court of the emperor. There was the "judge" in the left and the "guard" on the right. "There are three stars called *Sheti* at each side." *Sheti* referred to the constellations pointed by the dipper arm and could be used to indicate seasons. Here, they were compared to the ones who assist the emperors to divide seasons. In this way, the author described a scene of an authoritative court. From the "central palace" to the "eastern palace", the readers can know more than 160 stars under the guidance of Sima Qian.

The "southern palace" sat at the left and right sides of the ecliptic, namely the track of the solar annual apparent motion. Therefore, the sun, the moon and the major five stars frequently appeared in the "palace." So, Sima Qian called it the "court of three lights". The constellations were named to represent the generals and ministers,vassals, lords and scholar-officials. There was also Xuanyuan, which was compared to the "female ruler", namely the queen. Sima Qian vividly described the shape of the "southern palace": "The *Liu Constellation* is like the mouth of a bird; the *Xing Constellation* consisting of seven stars is like the neck of the bird; the *Zhang Constellation* is like the crop of the bird; the *Yi Constellation* is like the wings of the bird; together, they form up a 'Vermilion Bird'. The queen on the earth is phoenix, while the queen in the sky is a big red phoenix." Such description keeps in line with the traditional saying of "four images" and connects the "central palace" and "eastern palace" in a unified way.

Sima Qian compared the "western palace" to the logistics and hunting place guarded by the White Tiger. There were the "garage", "food storage" and the "herding garden". Where to find the White Tiger? Sima Qian wrote, "The *Can Constellation* looks like a white tiger…Above it there are three small stars in triangle shape at the border area, looking like the head of the white tiger."

Similar with the other "palaces", the "northern palace"

The Cowherd and the Weaving Girl story

125

was also made part of the society in the sky, and many of its constellations maintained the original names. Sima Qian said the Vega was the "granddaughter" of the "emperor" and compared the five stars of the *Wang Liang Constellation* into the "driver" of the "emperor". There was the "horse" by the "driver". Sima Qian described a scene of Wang Liang driving the horse carriage. It is interesting that, Sima Qian also imaged that the scene that the "emperor" went to attend worship ceremonies. He compared the South Dipper to the temple and *Niu Constellation* to the sacrificial offering.

Although the system of Chinese constellations of Sima Qian features strong literary flavor, it is different from the constellation myths of the ancient Greece. The latter includes a number of separated myths, which do not form up an integrated system. The constellation system of Sima Qian is an integrated system and there are connections between the five palaces. Of course, it reflects the centralized feudal system established in the Qin and Han dynasties. On the other hand, the Greek constellation myths do not include specific descriptions on fixed stars, while the constellation system in the chapter of *Astronomy* is about the stars, not only including the descriptions about the position of the fixed stars but also including specific star identification methods.

The chapter of *Astronomy* is like a guide map leading the readers to identify the stars, a mythonarrative poem telling the truth in a mysterious way and a precious and significant biography of stars and star constellations. Sima Qian ended the situation with different astronomical systems established in the Warring States period and inherited the achievements of the ancestors in identification of fixed stars and created an integrated constellation system. This effectively promoted the study on the movements of the sun, the moon and the five major five stars and made great contribution to the development of the astronomy of the ancient China. Today, when reading the *Records of the Grand Historian*, we should not forget his contribution in astronomy.

The *Records of the Grand Historian and* The *History of the Han Dynasty*

Zhu Ziqing

Both the *Records of the Grand Historian* and *The History of the Han Dynasty* are widely known in China. There are two reasons. First, both of them were the earliest systematic historical works. There were *The Book of Documents, The Spring and Autumn Annals of Lu (Lu Chun Qiu), The Discourses of the States, The Commentary of Zuo* and *The Strategies of the Warring States* before them. However, *The Book of Documents, The Discourses of the States* and *The Strategies of the Warring States* are all records of words but not records of history. *The Spring and Autumn Annals of Lu* and *The Commentary of Zuo* are records of history. However, the former is two simple and short, while the latter lacks systematic organization.The *Records of the Grand Historian* then became a pioneer work for biographical works. It covers a history of more than 3,000 years from the Yellow Emperor to the period under the reign of Emperor Wu of Han Dynasty, when the author lived. *The History of the Han Dynasty* adopts the form of the *Records of the Grand Historian*, but just covers a history of 230 years from the reign of Emperor Gaozu of Han Dynasty to the reign of Wang Mang. All the later historical books followed the style of *The History of the Han Dynasty*, meaning that they are all dynastic histories. Both the two works can be recognized as the origins of "official histories". Second, both the two works are literary classics. They have many similarities but more differences. Generally speaking, from the Eastern Han Dynasty to the Wei, Jin and Tan dynasties, more people liked *The History of the Han Dynasty*, but after the Tang Dynasty, more people liked the *Records of the Grand Historian*, especially in the Ming and Qing dynasties. This is because each of them has its own merits. However, in many cases, the two works were mentioned together, because they were written by using very similar narration and depiction skills.

The *Records of the Grand Historian* was written by Sima Qian (the fifth year of the Zhongyuan period under the reign of Emperor Jing (145 B.C. to ?), who was born in Xiayang City of Zuopingyi (currently Hancheng County, Shaanxi) and had a style name of Zichang. He is the son of Sima Tan, who once served as *Taishiling*. The young Sima Qian did farm work and herded cattle before moving to the capital city (current Xi'an) with his father. He began to read ancient books when he was 10 years old. After 20, he began to travel around the country. He visited the areas which are the currently Hebei, Shandong, Jiangsu and Zhejiang in the east, Hunan, Jiangxi, Yunnan and Guizhou in the south, Shaanxi, Gansu and Xikang in the west, and the Great Wall in the north. He nearly walked all over the country of Han, except for several newly established counties. Concerning the reason for his travel, some people said that his father asked him to collect historical materials, while some people said that he was on a business trip. There are no specific records on how many materials he collected. However, it is sure that he saw many ancient relics and heard many anecdotes, which were visual historical materials that proved and supplemented what he had learnt. That's why he could write the *Records of the Grand Historian* in a so cordial and insightful way. His travel experiences not only expanded his knowledge but also broadened his mind. He epitomized a history of more than 3,000 years into a book with extremely changeful writing skills. This shows how broad-minded he was.

Later, he passed the imperial examinations and held the official position of *Langzhong* in his twenties. In 110 B.C., Emperor Wu of Han Dynasty decided to hold a great ceremony to offer sacrifices to heaven. So, he led 180,000 subordinates and attendants to travel thousand miles to the site for the ceremony. As an official historian, Sima Tan should have accompanied the emperor to finish the trip. However, since he was very ill at that time, Sima Qian took over his position.Later, when Sima Qian got back, his father was going to die. The father held his son's hands and said, "From the reigns of Shun and Yu to the later period of the Zhou Dynasty, many generations of our family had worked as official historians. Then, we stopped holding the position and the family had been declining. I resumed the position but did not make any achievements. See, I even could not accompany the emperor to attend the ceremony. It must be the fate! We know that Confucius began to collect documents, edit *The Book of Songs* and *The Book of Documents* and write the *Spring and Autumn Annals* because he saw that there was no benevolent government and the traditional rites were abandoned. Therefore, he made immortal contributions. So far, more than 400 years have passed. The states are engaged in wars and many historical works have been lost. These materials should be collected and processed. In addition, the whole country has been unified, and the wise and able emperors and vassals,

莫大枵殺已降此乃將軍所已不得侯者也

餘人詐而同日殺之至今恨獨此耳朔曰禍

乎廣曰吾為隴西守羌嘗反吾誘降者八百

吾相不當侯耶朔曰將軍自念豈嘗有恨者

為後人然終無尺寸功已得封邑者何也豈

下村能不及中以軍功取侯者數十人廣不

漢擊匈奴廣未嘗不在其中而諸妄校尉已

更及士卒或取封侯廣与望氣王朔語曰自

下遠甚然廣不得爵邑官不過九卿廣之軍

He Shaoji's calligraphy on *the Religious Sacrificial Ceremonies* (part)

132

the loyal officials and the dead heroes should be recorded. I
have not fulfilled my duties as a historian and cannot leave
some works to the later generations. This makes me very
anxious. If you can take over my position and achieve my
unaccomplished aspiration and make a name, you will be a
filial son. You should remember my words." [1] Hearing what
his father said, Sima Qian cried and said, "I will carefully
process the materials you have collected to avoid losing
them." [2] Sima Tan died in the year when Sima Qian was 36
years old. However, the father directed a great road for his
son.

Three years after his father's death, Sima Qian was
appointed *Taishiling*. Then, he got the chance to read many
historical works and other kinds of books. Therefore, he
began to collect and process historical materials. Thanks to
his position, he had many historical materials, especially the
reports of the local administrations of the Han Dynasty.
He collected the materials at the same time of making the
calendars. Then, he began to write the book in the first
year of the Taichu Period (104 B.C.). In the second year
of the Tianhan period under the reign of Emperor Wu
of Han Dynasty (99 B.C.), receiving the order of Ershi
General Li Guangli, Li Ling led 5,000 soldiers to fight
against the Huns. They were besieged by 80,000 Huns.
Although they killed more than 10,000 Huns, more than
half of them had died. They put up a strong resistance for
eight days, without arrows and food, expecting the Ershi

General would send army to rescue them. However, the reinforcements did not come. Then, the Huns sent envoys to summon them to surrender. Feeling so shameful to come back, Li Ling agreed to surrender. Emperor Wu of Han Dynasty burst into anger after hearing the news. The officials defamed Li Ling in the court. The emperor asked Sima Qian's opinions on Li Ling. As a colleague of Li Ling, Sima Qian knew him well.

Sima Qian said that Li Ling was an allegiant official, who would like to sacrifice himself to safeguard the country. His troops killed so many enemies even when being hopelessly outnumbered. He did not fear death. So, his surrender must be a disguise so that he could get the chance to continue to serve the Han Dynasty. Hearing this, the emperor believed that Sima Qian was attributing the merits to Li Ling but not the Ershi General appointed by him in person. So, he ordered people to put Sima Qian in prison. The next year, the emperor killed all the members of Li Ling's family and punished Sima Qian with castration, which was a great insult. Sima Qian was very disappointed. However, he did not give up writing and even worked harder to finish his book, expecting to leave to a fine reputation in the future. Two years later, the emperor changed the reign title and announced an amnesty. Sima Qian was released and appointed *Zhongshuling* (an official position for eunuchs) later. Even with suffering mentioned above, he had never stopped writing his book, which was

Portrait of General Li Guang of Han Dynasty

finished in 91 B.C., with totally 130 chapters, including 526,500 Chinese characters. After his death, parts of the book were passed down. By the period under the reign of Emperor Xuan of Han Dynasty, Yang Yun, grandson of Sima Qian, submitted the book to the court and then the book was made public. In the Han Dynasty, it was named *The Book of Taishigong*, the *Taishigong*, *The Records of Taishigong* and *Taishi Ji* early. Then, to the Wei and Jin dynasties, it was renamed the *Records of the Grand Historian*. Some parts of the book were lost. The book today includes some supplements and manipulations. It is known that Chu Shaosun made some supplements to the book during the reigns of Emperor Yuan and Emperor Cheng. The other people who made supplements to it are unknown.

Inwardly, Sima Qian compared himself with Confucius. The latter was the first person to preserve the literatures at the end of the Zhou Dynasty, when many literatures were going to be lost. Sima Qian was the first person to preserve the literatures after the book burning movement in the Qin Dynasty. They have the same purpose though they adopted different ways to do the same thing. *The Preface of Shi Ji* recorded the discussion between Sima Qian and Hu Sui on writing histories. During the discussion, Sima Qian quoted his father's words to praise Confucius for collecting and processing the six classics and writing *The Spring and Autumn Annals*. Both Sima Qian and his father believed that Confucius wrote *The Spring and Autumn Annals*. He then quoted Dong Zhongshu's quotation of Confucius' words: "I have the ideal to awaken the people and save the world. However, I am afraid of that nobody will listen to me. So, it is better to refer to the historical facts to express my aspiration. It will be more inspiring and convictive." [3] It is just the interest and purport of Confucius to write *The Spring and Autumn Annals*: to show clearly the ways of governance, take proper attitude on the social affairs, distinguish the right and wrong and the good and evil, the virtuous and unworthy, revitalize the country and the noble families and make up the disadvantages and resume the abandoned to provide references for the later emperors and officials. *The Spring and Autumn Annals* is indeed a book about rites and morality. So, Sima Qian must believe that ruling by rites was more effective than ruling by law. He believed that *The Spring and Autumn Annals* was all-inclusive and it highlighted goodness and degraded evilness instead of sarcasm. As his father said, it is their responsibility to record and praise the emperors, sages, noble houses and officials with great virtue and contributions since the establishment of the Han Dynasty. His book has detailed records of the history of the Han Dynasty. This is partly due to the sufficiency of the historical materials, but also should be due to the author's respect to the contemporary. Sima Qian criticized the tyranny of the Qin Dynasty and expected that the Han Dynasty could last forever. It is like that *The Spring and Autumn Annals* embraces the Confucianism. So, his book was written by following the example of *The Spring and Autumn Annals*. Although Sima Qian said that he "just wanted to promote the inheritance of the six classics and collect the opinions of different schools", [4] and just write down the facts without creation and dared not to compare with *The Spring and Autumn Annals*, it was just modest words.

In *A Letter to Ren An*, Sima Qian wrote: "It is also

purpose to explore the relationship between the nature and the human society and show the historical changes through the ages, and to create the philosophy of my own."In *The Preface of Shi Ji*,he said, "I should collect the lost anecdotes, trace the origin for the rising of the emperors, watch the declines as well as the prosperities and verify the facts." Here, to trace the origin for the rising of the emperors and watch the declines as well as the prosperities is to show the historical changes through the ages and also explore the relationship between the nature and the human society, which means to figure out the influence of the nature on the people's world. Just as the intention to watch the declines as well as the prosperities, they are all the opinions of the Yin-Yang School, which believes that the declines and proprieties are decided by the movements of the five elements (metal, wood, water, fire and earth). The opinions of the Yin-Yang School especially prevailed in the Western Han Dynasty and integrated with the New Text Confucianism. Sima Qian had consulted Dong Zhongshu, who was a master in the New Text Confucianism. So, the latter may have some influence on him. The opinion of the Yin-Yang School on the five elements was originally part of the philosophy of history. It is actually to ask people to follow the natural tendency and cultivate morality.

Although the *Records of the Grand Historian* follows the example of *The Spring and Autumn Annals*, it was not written in a way nit-picking on words. Instead, it is a book of historical records, which allows the readers to distinguish what's good and what's evil. It indeed includes the author's comments, which are actually the complaints of the authors, generally making no difference. Since being involved in the case of Li Ling and punished by castration, Sima Qian had been working hard to write the book, because it was the only way to give vent to his depression. In *A Letter to Ren An* and *The Preface of Shi Ji*, he quoted a number of sages from King Wen of Zhou Dynasty to Hanfeizi, who were all representatives of people to write books to express their feelings, just as he did. The variable nature and world triggered his exclamation; he bemoaned the state of the universe and pitied the fate of humankind so that he expressed his complaints in his writings. This made his writing more sentimental. That is one of the reasons why the later generations like the book so much.

Concerning comments on earlier historical works, Ban Biao said, "(Sima Qian) made superficial and opinionated comments. He embraced the opinions of the Yellow Emperor and Lao-Tzu but belittled the five classics. He mentioned the biographies of the usurers in his work but undervalued the kindheartedness and justice and shamed the poor. He wrote about the knight-errants, indicating that he despised traditions but praised vulgar deeds." Ban Biao believed "that went against the right way". [5] Ban Gu also said that Sima Qian's views on right and wrong went against the sages'. [6] Actually, it was Sima Tan who

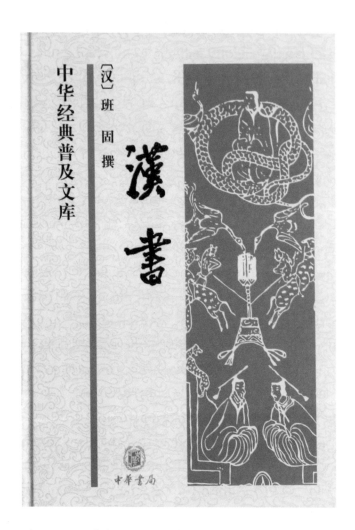

Photocopy of The *History of the Han Dynasty*

embraced the Taoist thoughts. By the period when Sima Qian lived, Confucianism had held the dominant position. Under such a circumstance, it was not strange that he became an embracer of the Confucianism. He wrote the *Biographies of Knight-errants* and the *Biographies of Usurers* because due to his personal experiences.At that time, people could atone for their crimes with money. Since Sima Qian had no money, he suffered heavy punishment. That's why he wrote about the usurers. While he was in an awkward and poor situation, no one dared to save or even speak for him. That's why he praised the knight-errants. It is similar with the question on the variable nature in the *Biography of Bo Yi*, just making use of a subject to elaborate the author's own ideas, without serious influence on the overall tenet of the book. Knowing that the author wrote the book to express his feelings, Wang Yun (Eastern Han Dynasty) made picky comments on the book, saying that it was a slanderous book written by a treacherous court official. [7] It was not only a misunderstanding of the book but also an undervaluing of Sima Qian.

The *Records of the Grand Historian* includes 12 chronological royal annals to record the political achievements of the emperors, 10 historical tables with brief records by year, eight monographs to record the development of ancient laws and regulations, 30 genealogies of noble houses to record the emerging and decline of the marquis-states and 70 biographies to record people in different fields. The historians call it a "biographical work", because "biographies" compose the most important part of the book. Before the *Records of the Grand Historian*, ancient historical works were just miscellaneous notes on parts of history or chronologically compiled records; the *Records of the Grand Historian* created a new mode to compile historical materials. Sima Qian made a success in integrating the Confucian classics and commentaries on them and the opinions of different schools to create the philosophy of his own. He knew the importance of good organization as well as how to do it: it was really creation, which was based on narration. He wrote the stories of the emperors, officials, gentries and ordinary people in the past 3,000 years into one book to reflect the great unification in the Qin and Han dynasties. *The Commentary of Zuo* is also a general history, but the *Records of the Grand Historian* is the first general history of certain scale. Ban Gu, son of Ban Biao, followed his father's opinions and said that "(Sima Qian) is a talented historian, who is good at narration, justification without rhetoric, simple and unsophisticated expression without vulgarness as well as direct and faithful record of history". [8] *The Records of the Grand Historian* has 130 chapters, half of which are biographies. The history of Sima Qian centers on the people. He was good at description. Under his pen, many important historical figures were vividly shown.

Ban Gu (A.D. 32 to A.D. 92), author of *The History*

of the Han Dynasty, with a style name of Mengjian, was born in Anling, Fufeng (currently Xianyang, Shaanxi). Just as Sima Qian, he was born in a family holding high official positions for generations, and he carried forward his father's aspiration. He was luckier than Sima Qian. His great-grandfather Ban Liu was erudite and talented. He proofread the royal books together with Liu Xiang in the period under the reign of Emperor Cheng. The emperor granted him with the whole set of royal books, including the *Records of the Grand Historian*. At that time, books were rarely spread among the ordinary people. So many scholars, such as Yang Xiong, visited the Ban's house to read these books. Ban Biao, grandson of Ban Liu, got the chance to read many books and communicate with many scholars. Later, he was engaged in study on Confucianism and became a historian. Although there were many historical works following the *Records of the Grand Historian*, many of them were prejudiced or philistine. Ban Biao then wrote the 65-chapters *Later History* (*Hou Zhuan*) by processing the earlier materials and making supplements to them. He gave specific comments on the successes and failures of the *Records of the Grand Historian*, which were usually correct and proper. His book only includes royal annals and biographies, and genealogies of noble houses were made part of the biographies. Unfortunately, the book was not passed down to the later generations, except that his son Ban Gu wrote *The History*

Portrait of Ban Gu

of the Han Dynasty based on it.

Ban Gu was born in Hexi area (currently northwestern Gansu). He had a little brother named Ban Chao and a little sister named Ban Zhao, who both made great contributions to the writing of *The History of the Han Dynasty*. At the age of five, Ban Gu and his father went to Luoyang, then capital of the country. At the age of nine, he began to write articles and read poems and proses. At the age around 16, he entered the college in Luoyang, where he got the chance to read many books. He learnt knowledge of different schools, focusing on the meaning and significance of the works instead of the wording. He was good at writing sentimental or descriptive compositions. He was gentle and generous, without arrogance. He studied in the college for seven years and went back to Anling at the age of 23, after his father died. In the first years of Yongping period under the reign of Emperor Ming of Han Dynasty (A.D. 58), at the age of 28, Ban Gu began to amend and compile his father's book. Believing that the *Later History* was not specific enough, he decided to write a great historical book. Three years later, he was accused of rewriting the history without approval and mongering rumors.

Emperor Ming ordered the officials of Fufeng County to arrest him and then put him in the prison in Luoyang. The emperor also read the manuscripts of Ban Gu. In the fifth year of the Yongping Period (A.D. 62), Ban Chao went to Luoyang and submitted a memorial to the emperor to make explanations and asked for meeting with the emperor. The emperor agreed to meet with Ban Chao. Bao Chao told the emperor that Ban Gu dared not to rewrite the history without approval and he just continue the work of their father.At that time, the emperor had read the manuscripts and liked them very much. So, he appointed Ban Gu *Jiaoshulang* and *Lantailingshi* (official titles) to amend the annals of Emperor Guangwu in cooperation with several other officials. At that time, the Ban's family was very poor. Bao Chao also worked to help his elder brother to support the family. Later, Ban Gu and some other people wrote 28 biographies of officials, which were made part of the *History of Later Han Dynasty (Dong Guan Han Ji)* compiled by Liu Zhen and other historians. These biographies have nothing to do with *The History of the Han Dynasty*.

At this time, Emperor Ming ordered Ban Gu to finish the book. In the seventh year of the Yongping Period (A.D.64), when Ban Gu was 33 years old, he resumed the work to write the book at Lantai, where the books of the royal family were kept. The next year, Ban Chao was also appointed *Lantailingshi*. He must have provided a lot of assistance to his brother. Emperor Zhang, who succeeded to the throne later and loved sentimental or descriptive compositions, also appreciates the talent of Ban Gu very much. Therefore, Ban Gu got the chance to read the books kept in the palace. Sometimes, he even read day and night. Around the seventh year of the Jianchu Period (A.D. 82), 51-year-old Ban Gu finished the book. In the first year of the Yongyuan period under the reign of Emperor He (A.D. 89), Cheji General Dou Xian led the army to fight against the Huns. He designated Ban Gu *Zhonghujun* (military official title) to participate in the making of military plans. The army defeated the Huns. Dou Xian order to make stone inscriptions on Yanran Mountain and asked Ban Gu to write the inscriptions, which became a well-known work later.

The next year, Ban Gu got back to the capital city

and began to work as a secretary of Dou Xian. Dou Xian had great power and influence. Although Ban Gu never took advantage of his position to bully people, his son and servants became bullies relying on the power of Dou Xian and thus offended many local officials, though these officials dared not to complain at that time. Once a servant got drunk and abused Chong Jing, head of Luoyang. Chong Jing was very angry. In the fourth year of the Jiyuan Period (A.D. 92), Dou Xian committed suicide after failing to murder Emperor He. Some of his followers were killed, while some were removed from their positions. Ban Gu was one of latter. Taking the chance to revenge, Chong Jing ordered to arrest Ban Gu and put him in prison. Then, Ban Gu was 61 years old. He could not stand the suffering in the prison and died soon. After hearing about the death of Ban Gu, Emperor He reprimanded Chong Jing and ordered to punish the responsible officials. By the time that Ban Gu died, The *History of the Han Dynasty* had not been organized well. So, the emperor ordered Ban Zhao, the little sister of Ban Gu who was erudite and respected due to high morality, to process the book. In addition, ten scholars were designated to study on the book. Ma Rong, a master in study on Confucian classics, was one of them. At that time, the eight tables and the treatise of astronomy had not been finished. Ban Zhao and the brother of Ma Rong finished them by using the royal books as references.

Ban Gu named the book *The History of the Han*

Dynasty. He gave the reason that, there had been the records of the reigns of Yao and Shun and the Xia, Shang and Zhou dynasties to praise the merits and virtues of emperors, but the Han Dynasty was not recorded until the reign of the sixth emperor, when Sima Qian wrote the *Records of the Grand Historian*, which, however, was a general history with the annals of the emperors of the Han Dynasty made a later part of the royal annals and equivalents to descendants of Yao, the emperors of Qin and Xiang Yu. He believed that it was not enough to highlight the position of the Han Dynasty. In addition, the *Records of the Grand Historian* ends with history of the reign of Emperor Wu of Han Dynasty, without mentioning of the following history. Therefore, he wrote the dynastic history covering a period of 230 years from Emperor Gaozu to the death of Wang Mang during the reign of Emperor Ping, with totally 100 chapters, including 12 annals, eight tables, 10 records and 70 biographies.[9] Although Ban Gu wrote the book based on his father's comments and the work seemed to be a supplement to the *Records of the Grand Historian*, it was his own creative idea to write a dynastic history. In this way, he carried forward the merits and virtues of the contemporary dynasty at the same time of preserving the historical literatures. Therefore, the book became an example for the later official histories. The creative idea of Ban Gu has great influence. It enables his book to have a wider coverage than the *Records of the Grand Historian*, including the nature, ghosts and gods, man and society, politics, art and literature.

The History of the Han Dynasty does not include independent genealogies of noble houses. The reason can be traced back to the *Later History* by Ban Biao. At that time, the Han Dynasty had established the feudal system without marquis-states. Therefore, there were not noble houses. This part was integrated into the biographies. The "records" in *The History of the Han Dynasty* were equivalent to the"treatises" in *Records of the Grand Historian*. The chapter of *Records of Art and Literature* (*Yi Wen Zhi*) was added to tell the ancient academic origin and development and the catalogue of the royal books. It was written based on the *Seven Abstracts* by Liu Xin. Liu Xiang and his son Liu Xin once proofread and sorted the royal books and made catalogues for them under the imperial edicts [10] so that these books can be widely spread. However, their original works had been lost, except for a major part of the *Seven Abstracts* quoted in the *Records of Art and Literature*, which became a treasury for the later bibliographers. After the book burning movement in the Qin Dynasty, many books were not appear again until the reign of Emperor Cheng of Han Dynasty, who issued an edict to collect the lost books nationwide. Then, these books were kept in the imperial palace. Obviously, it was then circumstance that promoted Liu Xiang and his son to make the catalogues and Ban Gu to add the *Records of Art and Literature* in his book.Compared with them, Sima Qian was not so lucky.

The *Records of the Grand Historian* was written by one person, while *The History of the Han Dynasty* was written by four people. The tables and records were written by Ban Zhao and Ma Xu; the annals and biographies from Emperor Zhao to Emperor Ping of Han Dynasty were written based on the *Later History* by Ban Biao, while those from Emperor Gaozu to Emperor Wu were written based on the *Records of the Grand Historian*. Therefore, it seems that there are quite a few of works written by Ban Gu himself. Some people said that his book was a plagiarism [11] instead of a work. However, at that time, there was no clear concept of "copyright" and therefore no awareness of plagiarism. Moreover, the history cannot be fabricated. Ban Gu deleted and proofed some earlier content, just following the principle to narrate without creation. What should be noticed is that, his deletion and proofing indicate his ingenuity. He didn't deal with the historical materials in a hasty way. The incomplete and obscure historical records of the Han Dynasty were made specific and clear by him. He spared no efforts to praise the wise and able emperors, sages, loyal officials and dead heroes. The book includes many others' articles so that some people said Ban Gu was an ostentatious person. [12] Most of these articles were

Ban Zhao

classics about politics and literature. Considering that there was no collection of works at that time, it might be a purpose of Ban Gu to preserve the historical materials. Concerning the reason for including the sentimental or descriptive compositions in the book, it must be related to then academic atmosphere and his own interests. However, from the modern perspective, these works are also literary and historical materials, which should not be neglected.

The debate on the merits and demerits of the two books by Ban Gu and Sima Qian started from the *On Balance* (*Lun Heng*) by Wang Chong, who said that the works of Ban Gu and his father boasted profound meaning, good structure and specific and clear narration and were better than the *Records of the*

Grand Historian. [13] Wang Chong embraced the principle for integration of rhetorical and substantial writing. [14] Sentimental or descriptive compositions prevailed in the Han Dynasty. So, the *Records of the Grand Historian*s includes many proses. However, *The History of the Han Dynasty* shows strong characteristics of parallelism and antithesis and includes many long sentences. This indicates the influence of the sentimental or descriptive compositions. To the Tang Dynasty, generally, the scholars liked *The History of the Han Dynasty* much more that the *Records of the Grand Historian*. Some scholars even dedicated to learning and studying The *History of the Han Dynasty*. This reflects the popularity of rhythmical prose characterized by parallelism and ornateness at that time. After the Tang Dynasty, proses gradually prevailed so that the *Records of the Grand Historian* became popular.Both Gui Youguang (a scholar of the Ming Dynasty) and the Tongcheng School scholars thought highly of the *Records of the Grand Historian*. The debate actually should be due to the differences of the two books in style and wording, which were changed according to what prevailed contemporarily.

Zhang Fu of Jin Dynasty disliked *The History of the Han Dynasty*. He said, "Many people believed that the work by Ban Gu was better than that by Sima Qian. However, Sima Qian wrote about the history of 3,000 years with about 500,000 Chinese characters, while Ban

Gu wrote about the history of about 200 years with 800,000 Chinese characters. In terms of the conciseness and clarity of language, how far Ban Gu is left behind by Sima Qian!" [15] Liu Zhiji wrote in his *Comments on Historical Records* that, "Although the *Records of the Grand Historian* is about a history of 3,000 years, only a history of more than 70 years of the Han Dynasty was detailed. The earlier part of the book is sketchy, while the later part is detailed. It is unbalanced. If Sima Qian wrote *The History of the Han Dynasty*, the book should be much longer. [16] Liu Zhiji had a bias towards Ban Gu so that his criticism was exaggerated.In all fairness, *The History of the Han Dynasty* is more expatiatory than the *Records of the Grand Historian*. The latter is a general history aiming to honor the Han Dynasty. Therefore, the author wrote about the early history in a sketchy way and the latest history in a detailed way. However, the writings about the history were not too detailed, because Sima Qian knew that it needed "balance". *The History of the Han Dynasty* is a dynamic history based on abundant historical materials to eulogize the merits and virtues of the Han Dynasty. Since it includes so many historical records, it is not strange that the book is too expatiatory. In addition, *The History of the Han Dynasty* includes more quotations than the *Records of the Grand Historian* does, and it is marked by parallelism and ornateness, with longer sentences than that in proses. They should not be deemed as defects of

The History of the Han Dynasty. Fan Ye wrote in *The History of the Later Han Dynasty: Postscript to the Bibliography of Ban Gu (Hou Han Shu: Ban Gu Zhuan Zan):* "The work of (Ban Gu) is not extreme or grotesque, without intentional excessive belittlement or compliment. It is based on abundant but well-organized materials. It is detailed but meets certain standard on writing style. That's why the readers are interested in it." It is the fact.

Zheng Qiao (Song Dynasty) criticized Ban Gu in his *General Records: Foreword,* almost equal to saying that Ban Gu's work was worthless. Liu Zhiji believed that dynamic histories were better than general histories, because general histories usually covered a long history

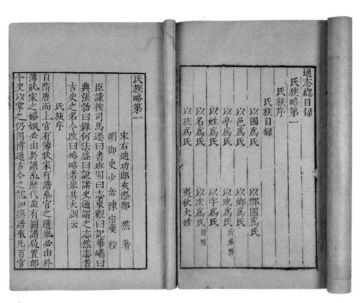

Photocopy of *General Records*

and the historical materials were incomplete so that the works always followed a set routine instead, hardly with new things. The *Records of the Grand Historian* also has the problem. There were many imitation works later, which were so redundant and multifarious to read. [17] In his opinion, works such as *The Spring and Autumn Annals of Lu* were just records of part of an era and equal to the records of the Han Dynasty in the *Records of the Grand Historian*; some of them were without beginning and end, or with beginning but without end.So, they could not compared with the dynamic histories, which recorded a historical period. Take *The History of the Han Dynasty* as an example, the records are all about the times when Ban Gu lived. Therefore, it was easy to get the historical materials and, as long as the author made enough efforts, he could present something new so that the readers will be always interested in it. [18] Zheng Qiao held opposite opinions. He paid more attention to thorough understanding, because he believed that history was consecutive so that only with thorough understanding could the author clearly show the evolution track. General histories could give a full view of the history and inspire people to have more in-depth understanding of the history. He said that the *Records of the Grand Historian* was the only classic after the six classics and *The History of the Han Dynasty* by Ban Gu only recorded the history of the Han Dynasty without clear boundaries and evolution track so that it was only a fragment of history. [19] Actually, both general histories and dynamic histories have merits and demerits. Both Liu Zhiji and Zheng Qiao had prejudices.

Both the *Records of the Grand Historian* and *The History of the Han Dynasty* have unique styles of their own. The former boasts straightforward narration and high faithfulness to historical facts, while the latter boasts sufficient basis and detailed narration. [20] Sima Qian expressed his sentiments between the lines, while Ban Gu directly showed them. However, as to historical work, the book of Ban Gu may be more objective and appropriate. Mao Kun (Ming Dynasty)said, *"The History of the Han Dynasty* meets the rules and standards." [21] Zhang Xuecheng (Qing Dynasty) said, "The Bans followed the rules." [22] It means the same. Fu Xuan (Jin Dynasty) had the following comments on Ban Gu: "Concerning politics, (he) covered up the shortcomings of the leaders and criticized the loyal officials; concerning edification, (he) highlighted the flatterers and belittled the righteous."[23] This is related to the insights and consciousness of the author but not the sentiments. It cannot be compared with Sima Qian's *Biographies of Knight-errants* and the *Biographies of Usurers*, which indicate endless pain from the life experienced by the author. Therefore, we cannot say that the work of Ban Gu is not objective. To sum up, the two works are different in writing skills, connotations and selection and organization of materials. However, they also have similarities. For example, both of them were created based on a vast collection and careful selection of historical materials, and both of them feature elaborative organization and writing. It is no accident that both of them are deemed as good historical works.

Notes

1 2 3 4 Please see *The Preface of Shi Ji* for the original texts.

5   *The History of the Later Han Dynasty: Biography of Ban Biao*

6   *The History of the Later Han Dynasty: Postscript to the Bibliography of Sima Qian*

7   *The History of the Later Han Dynasty: Biography of Cai Yong*

8   The same with 6.

9   *The History of the Han Dynasty: Autobiography*

10   *Abstracts(Bie Lu)*, Liu Xiang

11 12 *General Records: Foreword*

13   *The Chapter on Extraordinary Talents (Chao Qi Pian)*. Here it was quoted in accordance with the original annotation to the *Comments on Historical Records: Appreciation (Shi Tong: Jian Shi)*. So, it is different with the common edition.

14   *The Chapter on Extraordinary Talents*

15   Please see *The Book of Jin: Biography of Zhang Fu(Jin Shu: Zhang Fu Zhuan)* for the original text.

16   Please see the *Comments on Historical Records: Miscellaneous Sources (Shi Tong: Za Shuo)*for the original text.

17 18 *Comments on Historical Records:Six Schools (Shi Tong: Liu Jia)*

19 *The same with (11)(12).*

20 *The History of the Later Han Dynasty: Postscript to the Bibliography of Ban Gu*

21 *Preface for Comments on The History of the Han Dynasty (Han Shu Ping Lin Xu)*

22 *General Interpretation of Historiography:Poem Moralization II (Wen Shi Tong Yi: Shi Jiao II)*

23 *Comments on Historical Records: Writing (Shi Tong: Shu Shi)*[Reference] Zheng Hesheng's *Study on the Records of the Grand Historian* and *The History of the Han Dynasty, The Chronicle of Sima Qian's Life, The Chronicle of Ban Gu's Life.*

Comparison of the *Records of the Grand Historian* and *The History of the Han Dynasty*

Qu Lindong

The *Records of the Grand Historian* and *The History of the Han Dynasty* are compared to the "Gemini" of the Han Dynasty and "two peaks" in the science of history of China, with great influence on the later generations. Therefore, it nearly has become a common view that Sima Qian and Ban Gu have the same status among the historians and both the two works play an important role in the historical literature. They have been the most popular targets of the later studies and received the most comments. There are even special studies on them. For more than 1,000 years, the two works have been compared by the people, who look for their similarities and differences and debate on which one is greater. It seems that they are permanent topics in the academic circle. In my opinion, there are three reasons for this: first, their high position in the science of history, which greatly attracts the people; second, the comparable elements in the two works; third, the enlightenment through the comparison. Then, how to compare them?

I. Start with *On Key Points of Six Schools* (Lun Liu Jia Yao Zhi) and *On Destiny of Throne* (*Wang Ming Lun*)

Both Sima Qian and Ban Gu, the authors of The *Records of the Grand Historian* and *The History of the Han Dynasty*, had the background of family schooling. By identifying the difference of such background, we can find the difference between then in writing purposes.

Sima Qian's father Sima Tan, who once served as *Taishiling* of the Western Han Dynasty, was a scholar with insightful academic opinions. He wrote the book named *On Key Points of Six Schools*, which gave comments on the merits and demerits of the six ideological schools of Yin-Yang, Confucianism, Mohism, Logics, Legalism and Taoism. The book shows the broad view and the open-mindedness of the author to carry forward the merits of

Portrait of Lao Tzu

different academic schools. The author quoted the sentence in the *Yi: Dazhuan*: "The people in the world achieve the same goals through the contention of different opinions and different roads lead to the same destination." Then, he wrote:

The schools of Yin-Yang, Confucianism, Mohism, Logics, Legalism and Taoism all target at realizing peace and prosperity, though they tried to achieve it by taking different ways. Some are obvious, while some are not. I made a study on the school of Yin-Yang and found that it focuses on omens for good and bad fortunes as well as weal and woe. It has many taboos, which restrict people and make them afraid. However, the school of Yin-Yang tells the running rules of the four seasons of a year, which should not be abandoned. The Confucianism boasts a wide coverage of knowledge but lacks essentials. Therefore, great efforts were made in an inefficient way so that it was rarely completely followed. However, the etiquettes between the ruler and his ministers and between the father and his son should not be changed. The Mohism school was too frugal so that it is hard to completely follow its opinions. However, its proposal to enhance agricultural production and economize expenses should not be abandoned. The Legalism school advocates severe law enforcement but treats the people harshly and gives rare generosity. However, its distinguishing of the positions of the ruler and his ministers should not be changed. The Logics school puts on restrictions on the people but loses the authenticity. However, its distinguishing of the name and the substance should be seriously studied. The Taoism tells people to focus and act in accordance with intangible natural rules to make all the things abundant. The opinions of the Taoism school are based on the opinions of the Yin-Yang school on the four seasons and absorb the merits of the Confucianism and Mohism schools and the essentials of the Logics and Legalism schools. It changes with the times to adapt to the changes of the world to set up good and proper customs for the people. It shows simple tenets that are easy to follow with fewer efforts.

The Confucianism is different. They believe the ruler is the leader of a country and the ministers should response to what the ruler advocates and follow what the ruler does. Therefore, the ruler is very busy, while his ministers live an easy and comfortable life. The Taoists believe that the toughness and desires should be abandoned and the wisdom should be given up to govern the country with strategies. The mind will be exhausted if it is overused, and the body will be tired if it is too busy.It is rarely heard that people with physical and spiritual disorders could live peacefully or exist as long as the nature does. (The Preface of Shi Ji)

The comment mentioned above indeed makes sense, except for overestimation of the Taoism, and gives a basic summarization of the characteristics of these schools. Sima Tan believed that each school had opinions acceptable and unacceptable. He suggested that people abandon what were unacceptable and carry forward what were acceptable to adapt to the changes along the time and do things in an efficient way. He thought it was a major issue that should be paid enough attention by then scholars.

On Key Points of Six Schools not only reflects the ideological origin of Sima Qian from his family, but also reflects the cultural background and academic environment for his creation of the *Records of the Grand Historian*. Attaching great importance to the work, Sima Qian quoted all the contents of *On Key Points of Six Schools* in *The Preface of Shi Ji*. Influenced by *On Key Points of Six* Schools, the author dared to give objective comments on different schools and people in the history and make profound exploration of the historical development and changes.

Different from Sima Tan, Ban Gu's father Ban Biao was born in a family with many books granted by the imperial family and good economic conditions. In the first year of the Jianwu period of the Eastern Han Dynasty (A.D. 25), when Ban Biao was 20 years old, the administration of Wang Mang failed and Liu Xiu proclaimed himself emperor in Jizhou and established the Eastern Han Dynasty. However, there were also other people proclaimed themselves emperors. Under such a circumstance, Ban Biao, who eagerly expected a rejuvenation of the Han Dynasty, wrote *On Destiny of Throne*, which includes two key points.(1) "The family of Liu (referring to the imperial family of the Han Dynasty) was in direct line of succession of Emperor Yao, and the genealogy of the family was recorded in *The Spring and Autumn Annals*; Yao has the virtue for imperial power and the Han Dynasty inherited it."(2) "It is the god's will to grant the emperors the power that cannot be obtained by wisdom and strategies; it is the destiny of the Han Dynasty to rule the country, which is not based on the people's will and efforts." (*The History of the Han Dynasty: Autobiography*). To sum up, it said that the Han Dynasty was in direct line of succession of

Emperor Yao and doomed to rule the country. Bao Biao was also telling the people that: it was the fate of the people to be rich or poor, and it depended on the people's will to have good or bad luck. He expected that the people could understand the importance of the rejuvenation of the Han Dynasty and did not oppose the court established by Liu Xiu. The historical fact that the ruling the Eastern Han Dynasty was consolidated later indicated that Ban Biao was right. However, it still cannot be denied that Ban Biao's views were idealistic.

Just as the influence of *On Key Points of Six Schools* on Sima Qian, the *On Destiny of Throne* has great influence on Ban Gu's writing. Ban Gu also quoted the full text of the *On Destiny of Throne* in T*he History of the Han Dynasty: Autobiography* and even made extension of the thoughts about the succession of the Han Dynasty from Yao's reign. To a large extent, this indicates the ideological origin of Ban Gu's idealistic and conservative views of history.

The difference in family schooling was decided by different historical environments. Sima Tan and Sima Qian lived in the period that the social and economic development of the Western Han Dynasty was recovering and speeding up and the political rule of the Han Dynasty was going stable after several crises.In addition, although Emperor Wu of Han Dynasty adopted the proposal of Dong Zhongshu to ban from hundred schools of thought to venerate Confucianism, the Confucianism had not been really accepted by the supreme rulers. Just as Emperor Xuan of Han Dynasty said, "The ruling family of the Han Dynasty has its own system and adopts miscellaneous governance strategies." (*The History of the Han Dynasty: Imperial Annals of Emperor Yuan of Han Dynasty*). Therefore, it was not strange that the *On Key Points of Six Schools* appeared. Ban Biao and Ban Gu lived in a period that the new dynasty was being established and consolidated through a number of significant historical events, such as the throne of Wang Mang and the peasants' uprising in later Western Han Dynasty. The supreme rulers were very eager to know how to safeguard their ruling. In addition, there were notable changes of the thoughts on ruling. From the Shiquge Meeting held at the end of the reign of Emperor Xuan of Han Dynasty(51 B.C.) to the Baihuguan Meeting held in the early reign of Emperor Zhang (A.D. 79), the ministers and Confucian scholars discussed about the similarities and differences of the *Five Classics*, while the emperors made the conclusions. This enabled the further integration of the Confucianism and the theory that "man is an integral part of nature" and superstitions. The *On Destiny of Throne* was just a result of the times.

Both *On Key Points of Six Schools* and *On Destiny of Throne* had great influence on the creation of the *Records of the Grand Historian* and *The History of the Han*

Portrait of Emperor Yao

Dynasty. Therefore, the comparison of the differences of the two works and the historical conditions for the creation of the works becomes a precondition for the comparison of the _Records of the Grand Historian_ and _The History of the Han Dynasty_.

II. To show the changes and straighten out the history

This is a major difference between the thoughts of Sima Qian and Ban Gu.

In _A Letter to Ren An_, Sima Qian revealed his purposes to write the book:

I am trying to do something beyond my ability to use my insufficient writing skills to collect historical materials nationwide, briefly verify the facts and tell the truth, trying to find the reasons for the successes and failures as well as the prosperity and decline. Therefore, I wrote 130 chapters, including 12 royal annals, 10 tables, eight monographs, 30 genealogies of noble houses and 70 biographies, which cover the history from the Yellow Emperor to the contemporary era. It is also a purpose to explore the relationship between the nature and the human society and show the historical changes through the ages, and to create the philosophy of my own.

Here, the key points are to "explore the relationship between the nature and the human society and show the historical changes through the ages". It was for the first time that an ancient historian set such a goal for his creation.

168

It is a core thought of Sima Qian to show the historical changes through the ages. There had been related opinions in the ancient China. For example, "Any circumstance hitting a limit will begin to change. Change will in turn lead to an unimpeded state, and then lead to continuity." (*Book of Changes: Xi Ci II*). Sima Qian carried forward the opinions and manifested them with specific historical facts. Concerning his purposes to write the book, the first was to recognize the functions of the major changes throughout the historical development. For example, the changes included: the First Emperor of the Qin Dynasty merged the six states; Emperor Gaozu of Han Dynasty changed the systems and customs; Emperor Wen of Han Dynasty alleviated the excessive burdens or oppressive measures. The second was to make primitive exploration and observe the decline as well the prosperity, aiming to verify the facts of each historical period and find the clues for the decline of a dynasty from its flourishing age. So he said he wanted to briefly verify the facts and tell the truth, trying to find the reasons for the successes and failures. The third was to intentionally highlight the changes. For example, he wrote that: the *Rites* (*Li Shu*) basically conformed to the historical changes; the *Bells* (*Lv Shu*) corresponded with the recent history and reflected the changes; the *Equalization* (*Ping Zhun Shu*) was about the observation of the changes. The fourth was to highlight the continuity and changes through the history. He said that the book was to make a

First Emperor of the Qin Dynasty

brief inference on the Xia, Shang and Zhou dynasties and make specific records of the Qin and Han dynasties to cover the history from the reign of the Yellow Emperor to the contemporary era. These purposes were also clearly reflected in the preface of the 10 tables, though they were hardly discovered by the readers, who usually neglect these tables.

However, Ban Gu had different purpose to write *The History of the Han Dynasty*, namely to straighten out the history. In *The History of the Han Dynasty: Autobiography*, he wrote:

Being in direct line of succession of Emperor Yao, the Han Dynasty was established. To the reign of Emperor Wu of Han Dynasty, the historian (Sima Qian) wrote the royal annals to record the merits and virtues of the emperors. He ranked the emperors of the Han Dynasty after the emperors of other dynasties and apposed them with the Qin's emperor and Xiang Yu. Since there were no records of the history after the Taichu Era, I made researches on the early documents and collected materials to write The History of the Han Dynasty, which covers the history of 230 years, from Emperor Gaozu to time when Empress Xiaoping and Wang Mang were killed. The book gives a comprehensive narration of the historical events, makes reference to the Five Classics, and straightens out the history, with totally 100 chapters, including annals, tables, records and biographies.

This passage reflects the overall guiding thought of Ban Gu for writing the book. Yan Shigu (Tang Dynasty) made annotations for *The History of the Han Dynasty*. Referring to the purpose to "give a comprehensive narration of the historical events, make reference to the Five Classics, and straighten out the history", he annotated that: "It is why the tables and records written by Ban Gu were deemed as classics." He believed that these phrases reflected the purposes of Ban Gu to write the book. However, his views were not complete, because the annals and biographies in the book also reflected the purposes of the author.

Ban Gu set the purpose to straighten out the history to: (1) coordinate various factors based on wide range of knowledge (totally different with the purpose of Sima Qian to explore the historical changes); (2) use the *Five Classics* as the ideological and theoretical principles (This must be related to the status of Ban Gu as an attendee to the Baihuguan Meeting and a preparer of the *Memorial on Discussions at the Baihuguan Meeting* and is completely different with the principle of Sima Qian to briefly verify the facts and tell the truth, trying to find the reasons for the successes and failures as well as the prosperity and decline and the purpose to create the philosophy of his own.); (3) emphasize that the Han Dynasty is in direct line of succession of Emperor Yao and criticize Sima Qian for ranking the emperors of the Han Dynasty after the

emperors of other dynasties and apposing them with the
Qin's emperor and Xiang Yu.

To sum up, Sima Qian aimed to explore the historical
changes and followed the principle of observing the
history in an objective way to write the books. Ban Gu
aimed to prove that the Han Dynasty was in direct line of
succession of Emperor Yao and set the *Five Classics* as
the standards to evaluate the history. He only focused on
the Han Dynasty. Zhang Xuecheng, a Chinese historian
of the Qing Dynasty, said, "The book of Sima Qian shows
the historical changes, while that of Ban Gu sticks to
the rules and regulations." (*General Interpretation of
Historiography: Book Moralization II, Wen Shi Tong Yi:
Shu Jiao II*). It just gets to the point.

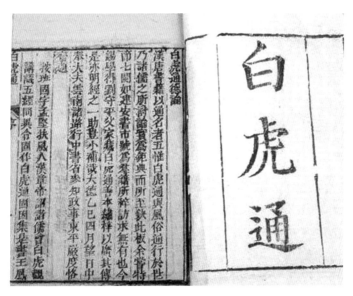

Photocopy of *Baihu Tongyi*

III. Flexible style and insightful opinions via normalized style and wide coverage of knowledge

Of the ancient scholars who had made comparison of the *Records of the Grand Historian* and T*he History of the Han Dynasty*, Liu Zhiji (Tang Dynasty) and Zhang Xuecheng (Qing Dynasty) were the most influential.In the *Comments on Historical Records: Six Schools* and the *Comments on Historical Records: Two History Recording Styles (Er Ti)*, Liu Zhiji criticized the *Records of the Grand Historian* but highly praised *The History of the Han Dynasty*, though he also made poignant remarks on the errors in the *The History of the Han Dynasty: Records of Five Elements (Wu Xing Zhi)*. Zhang Xuecheng said that Liu Zhiji's comments on historical books focused on the ways in which the work was written, while he himself focused on the meaning of the work (*General Interpretation of Historiography: Letter II*) (*Wen Shi Tong Yi: Jia Shu II*). Today, it is shown that, indeed, Zhang's comments were much more brilliant than Liu's. Referring to the evolution of the Chinese historical books, Zhang Xuecheng made a lot of comparisons of the two works. He said that:

There were some historical works after The Spring and Autumn Annals, and the works by Sima Qian and Ban Gu should be the most outstanding ones. The work by Sima Qian boasts flexible style and insightful opinions, while the one by Ban Gu boasts normalized style and wide coverage of knowledge.

The Spring and Autumn Annals by Zuo Qiuming was based on The Book of Documents, while the latter lacked organization and the former had normalized pattern; the annals and biographies of the Records of the Grand Historian by Sima Qian were based on the Spring and Autumn Annals, while the latter was chronological and the former made records by categories; the dynamic historical work by Ban Gu was based on the work by Sima Qian, while the latter shows the historical changes and the former sticks to the rules and regulations. In terms of the style and pattern, the work by Sima Qian is very different from the work by Zuo Qiuming, while the work by Ban Gu is similar with that by Sima Qian; Zuo Qiuming was the first to write annalistic work, while Sima Qian and Ban Gu were the first to write biographical historical works. In terms of the details of the works, the work by Sima Qian has close connections with the work by Zuo Qiuming, while the work by Ban Gu has less connections with the work by Sima Qian; therefore, the work by Sima Qian boasts flexible style and insightful opinions, most of which should be sourced from The Book of Documents, while the work by Ban Gu boasts normalized style and a wide coverage of knowledge, showing the great influence of The Rites of Zhou (Zhou Li). (General Interpretation of Historiography: Book Moralization II)

These quotations aim to repeat the characteristics of the two works: the *Records of the Grand Historian* boasts

Photocopy of *the Book of Changes*

flexible style and insightful opinions, while *The History of the Han Dynasty* boasts normalized style and a wide coverage of knowledge.

Zhang Xuecheng made comparison of the two works from three aspects. First, the *Records of the Grand Historian* shows the historical changes, while *The History of the Han Dynasty* sticks to certain rules and regulations. This is the difference in the author's purposes and principles. The second was the comparison of the types and forms of the two works. They are similar. Both of them were the earliest biographical historical works (The *Records of the Grand Historian* was the earliest general history presented in a series of biographies, while *The History of the Han Dynasty* was the earliest dynamic history presented in a series of biographies.) The third was the comparison of the ideological contents. He believed the *Records of the Grand Historian* was better than *The History of the Han Dynasty*, and the former boasted flexible style and insightful opinions, while the latter boasted normalized style and a wide coverage of knowledge. It contained two parts. The first was the comparison of the styles, where one was flexible and the other one was normalized. The second was the comparison of content, especially the difference in ideological background, where one had significant insights on the historical evolution and the other showed the author's good ability to store and organize historical knowledge.

Zhang's opinions are enlightening for today's study on the comparison of the two works.

Zhang Xuecheng's opinions on the comparison of the ideological contents were actually the extension of a traditional thought sourced from the *Book of Changes: Xi Ci I*. Zhang Xuecheng said that he borrowed its meaning to make summary of the ancient works. He divided a historical work into two parts: writings and records. He said, "The writings are flexible and reflect the style and thought of the author. The records follow certain rules and regulations based on a wide coverage of knowledge. The records were made to remember the history, while the writings were made to enlighten the later generations. Therefore, the records keep the history with knowledge, while the writings predict the future with insights. The records focus on completeness so that they follow certain rules and regulations, while the writings focus on the author's will so that they are flexible." (*General Interpretation of Historiography:Book Moralization II*) Based on that, Zhang Xuecheng believed that the *Records of the Grand Historian* was more flexible in style and insightful in ideology, while *The History of the Han Dynasty* was more normalized and informative. It is worth noting that it is basically right to evaluate the social functions of the two works in this way. Sima Qian once compared himself with his predecessors, saying that his purpose to write the work was to "tell the history and predict the future" (*The Preface of Shi Ji*). Ban Gu's purpose to write *The History of the Han Dynasty* was to demonstrate the legitimacy of the Han Dynasty and serve the governance and promote the prosperity of the country. (*The History of the Han Dynasty: Autobiography*) This is a main difference between the two works.

There are many discussions and studies on the comparison of the two works. This paper only focused on three major aspects. The comparison of the two works has been a subject of comparative study on history. Even today, it still has great value for study. Concerning the study methods, there are three points. The first is to read the treatises on these works from the latest ones to the ancient ones (such as the *New Opinions on the Records of the Grand Historian*,1981; the Essays o*n the Records of the Grand Historian*,1984; the *New Discussions on Study on Sima Qian*, 1982, Henan People's Publishing House; *Opinions of Famous Historians on the Records of the Grand Historian*, 1986).The second is to pay attention to macro comparison based on integration of micro and macro comparison. The third is to avoid bias but to make well-grounded and scientific evaluation of the works.

The *Records of the Grand Historian* in Japan

Qin Qixun

The Japanese historian circle has two views about when the *Records of the Grand Historian* was taken to Japan. One view is that the time is unknown. Ikeda Shirojiro wrote in his Views on References for the *Records of the Grand Historian: the Value of the Book in Japan* that, "When the *Records of the Grand Historian* by Sima Qian was taken to Japan is unknown." The second view is that the book was taken to Japan when the two countries began to send envoys to each other, as mentioned by Noguchi Sadao in *Reading the Records of the Grand Historian*. The results of the study on a great amount of Japanese data indicated that, the *Five Classics* had been spread to Japan before Mikado Suiko held the throne in A.D. 592, but the *Records of the Grand Historian* had not appeared by that time. In the following eight years under the reign of the Empress Suiko, there were still no objective conditions for the book to be taken to Japan. In A.D. 600, Prince Shotoku sent the first envoys to the Sui Dynasty. In A.D. 604, Prince Shotoku issued the *17-Article Constitution*, which indicated that the Japanese had made profound study on the *Records of the Grand Historian* and a number of Confucian classics. Therefore, the book should be taken to Japan by the first Japanese envoys to the Sui Dynasty from 600 to 604. Although there are no records of the spread of the *Records of the Grand Historian* in Japan in the following eras, the *Study on the Books Shipped to Japan during the Edo Period: Data* by famous Japanese scholar Ohba Osamu indicated that, 260 volumes of Chinese books, including 3,012 books, were taken to Japan during this period. Therefore, the Edo period, when the ancient China was under the reigns of the Ming and Qing dynasties, should be a golden age for the spread of the *Records of the Grand Historian in Japan*.

The *Records of the Grand Historian* had great influence on both the court and the commonalties of Japan after it was taken to Japan. After Suiko took the throne, Prince Shotoku proposed to call the Suiko "Mikado" (emperor or empress) instead of "king". It was derived from the *Records of the Grand Historian:Annals of Qin Shi Huang*. Michio Morishima wrote in *Why Has Japanese Succeeded?* that, Prince Shotoku created the word of "Mikado". Since then, the Mikados has become a symbol of the Japanese nation and the core for the cohesion of the nation. In A.D.604. Prince Shotoku integrated the Confucian concepts and the idea of grand feudal unity into the *17-Article Constitution*, which laid a significant foundation for the Taika Reform in A.D.645. In accordance with a number of Japanese historical works, such as the *Records of Three Generations*, the *Nihon Kiryaku* and the *Fuso Ryakki*, both Suiko and her successors liked to read the *Records of the Grand Historian*, especially Meiji. Records showed that, in the 10th years under the reign of Meiji, the emperor studied the *Records of the Grand Historian* on the 2nd, 7th, 12th, 17th, 22nd and 27th days of each month and read the *Comments on the Records of the Grand Historian (Shi Ji Ping Lin)*. In addition, in order to train political talents with good knowledge of foreign countries, the Japanese court organized scholars to make special studies on the *Records of the Grand Historian* and other historical works. Moreover, the royal family of Japan often granted the Records of the Grand Historian to the government departments so that the civil and military

Prince Shotoku

officials could study on it and learn experience for the governance of the Japanese society.

The *Records of the Grand Historian* also has great influence on the education of Japan, beginning with the influence on the royal education. This is directly reflected by the formulation of the *17-Article Constitution*, for which the *Records of the Grand Historian* was made part of the references. In the Nara and Heian periods, the book was used as textbook for the royal schooling. The *Pick up the Mustard* said that, after getting back to Japan, Kibi Makibi ordered to keep the Chinese historical books in special shelves and recruit students to learn these books. The Japanese government paid high attention to the learning of the *Records of the Grand Historian* so that many officials learnt the book well and even made poems about the content of the book. In accordance with related documents, General Tokugawa Ieyasu read the book and then highly praised Emperor Gaozu of Han Dynasty for his lenience and generosity. He also praised Zhang Liang, Han Xin, Sima Qian and the Duke of Zhou for their extraordinary talents.In addition, the book also played an important role in the education of the Buke family and the vassal schooling. Even in the modern times, it is still an important source for the Japanese textbooks to learn Sinology. For example, the book titled *On Theories and Practice of Colleges and Universities Under the Guidance of Classics* issued by Meiji Shoin on the 12th Day of the

10th Month of the 56th year of the Showa period quoted the article written by Inoue Tadashi, namely the *Guidance of the Records of the Grand Historian*, which included profound study on the content of the book, such as the stories about the small tricks by crowing like a cock and snatching like a dog.

The appearance of the *Records of the Grand Historian* in Japan marked the beginning of the spread of the Chinese science of history in Japan. Before that, Japan had no its own national history and science of history. The first and second Japanese national historical works, namely the *Kojiki* (the *Records of Ancient Matters*) and the *Nihon Shoki*, were finished in A.D.712 and 720. Although they are all annalistic works, both of them indicate the influence of the *Records of the Grand Historian*. For example, both of them start with myths and legends, center on the state leaders to make historical records and have structures arranged in chronological order. Then, with the increase of the Japanese scholars engaged in the study of the *Records of the Grand Historian*, a proficient team specializing in the study of the book was formed up.Preliminary estimates indicated that, there are 126 influential Japanese scholars engaged in the study of the book in the modern times. Of them, there are Takigawa Sukenobu, Mizusawa Toshitada, Miyazaki Ichisada, Noguchi Sadao, Kaji Nobuyuki and Ikeda Shirojiro. There are more than 680 types of related monographs and translations as well as numerous papers. The Japanese scholars' studies on the *Records of the Grand Historian* provide valuable experience. First, great importance should be attached to the translation of the book. In accordance with relevant Japanese data, Togen Zuisen, a well-known monk and scholar of Japan, wrote the T*ogen's Copy of the Records of the Grand Historian* from 1469 to 1487. The work consisting of 19 volumes has been recognized the earliest formal translation of the *Records of the Grand Historian*. There is another example, namely *The Translation of the Records of the Grand Historian* published in 1925. It is bilingual and easy to read. The annotations were based on the *Comments on the Records of the Grand Historian* by Ling Zhilong of the Ming Dynasty, the *Verification of the Records of the Grand Historian* (*Shi Ji Zhi Yi*) by Liang Yusheng of the Qing Dynasty and the *Extensive Comments on the Records of the Grand Historian* by Riken Nakai. Statistics showed that Japan has about 100 wholly translated and selectively translated versions of the *Records of the Grand Historian*. Various translations of the book provide favorable conditions for the Japanese people to learn the *Records of the Grand Historian*. Second, great importance should be attached to the explanations in the original book. In this aspect, Dr. Takigawa Sukenobu made the greatest contribution. In the *Research of the Annotations of the Records of* *the Grand Historian*, he explained his opinions based on comparison of the annotations of the *Records of the Grand Historian* of different academic schools. The work boasts careful emendation and well-grounded research. The *General Remarks on the Records of the Grand Historian* in the book features rich content and wise quotation of the original texts. The work provides convenience for the Japanese scholars to understand the context of the *Records of the Grand Historian* and clues for the Chinese scholars to learn about the Japanese scholars' study on the *Records of the Grand Historian*. That's why the *Research of the Annotations of the Records of the Grand Historian* was recognized as a greatly significant and influential work. Although there are some errors in the book, generally the defects cannot obscure the merits. Third, the biographies should be highlighted. Some people in the Japanese academic circle believe that the *Records of the Grand Historian* is a classic for exploring the human history. Therefore, many Japanese experts in related studies pay high attention to the study of the biographies in the book. Here the biographies refer to the annals, genealogies and biographies in the book. Fourth, collection of materials should be a main basis for scientific study. The remarkable achievements made by the academic circle of Japan in the studies of the Records of the Grand Historian should be due to the wide collection of historical materials. For example, the *Records of the Grand Historian*: the World of Sima Qian by Kaji Nobuyuki, the *Reading the Records of the Grand Historian* by Noguchi Sadao and the *On the Records of the Grand Historian* by Miyazaki Ichisada, are all based on abundant historical materials. In addition, the *Views on References for the Records of the Grand Historian* by Ikeda Shirojiro and his father Ikeda Hideo also boasts rich content, meticulous style design and wide coverage of knowledge, leaving many similar Chinese works far behind. We should learn the experience in collecting and applying historical materials from them.

The *Records of the Grand Historian* promoted the appearance of the earliest Japanese chronicles, which play an important role in the classical literature of Japan. Both the *Kojiki* and the *Nihon Shoki* are the most representative works, and both of them were greatly influenced by the *Records of the Grand Historian*. In addition, the *Records of the Grand Historian* also had great influence on other literatures. Moreover, the *Records of the Grand Historian* has profound relationship with the *Genji Monogatari*. In early 11th century, Murasaki Shikibu wrote the *Genji Monogatari*, which then becomes one of the most classical literatures of Japan. It was the personal experience of the author including the decline of her family, the death of her husband and the long-term personal experience of the royal life that set the stage for the great work. However, it is rarely known that Murasaki Shikibu was

Murasaki Shikibu is writing *Genji Monogatari*.

well educated by her family when she was young and had systematic learning of the R*ecords of the Grand Historian*. Therefore, her work has similar characteristics, namely rich sentiments, excellent descriptions and natural expression. Moreover, the author also directly borrowed the figure of Concubine Qi from the *Records of the Grand Historian* and created a similar figure of empress in her work to reveal the real Japanese society at that time and the complicated contradictions through exquisite conception and expression. What's more, the book also quoted many words and stories from the *Records of* *the Grand Historian*. Third, the *Records of the Grand Historian* has a prominent position in the field of Japanese poems in Chinese, which are recognized as a miracle in the classical literature of Japan. The poems were written in Chinese and imitated the rhythms of the Chinese poems of the Tang Dynasty. Many of them are directly themed on the experience of Sima Qian and the content of his work, with the characteristics of eulogizing the history, good application of rhythms, ingenious quotations and highlighting the *Records of the Grand Historian*. For example, in the *Bunka Shureishu*, which is a well-known collection of Japanese poems in Chinese, there are four poems to eulogize the history: the *On Zhang Zifang* by Emperor Saga, *On Ji Li* by Yoshimine no Yasuyo, *On Emperor Gaozu of Han Dynasty* by Naka Oō and *On Sima Qian* by Sugawara no Kiyotomo(See below).

The best author of history of the Han Dynasty should be Sima Qian, who was a genius born for the time. Who made prudent research of the history and wrote the masterpiece following the Spring and Autumn Annals by Confucius. With faithful records and objective comments, the work casts thousands of similar works into the shade and hold a leading position for a long time.

The *Records of the Grand Historian* has great influence on Japan. The history shows that there are no boundaries for excellent cultures, which belong to the same world and are precious spiritual wealth of the human society. There is no denying that the Japanese have done a better job in the study and rational inheritance of the *Records of the Grand Historian*. We should admit it and respect the reality so that we can do a better job.

图书在版编目(CIP)数据

名家讲《史记》：英文/《文史知识》编辑部编；王丽，李莉译.
—北京：五洲传播出版社，2016.1（中国文化经典导读）
ISBN 978-7-5085-3215-8

Ⅰ.①名… Ⅱ.①文… ②王… Ⅲ.①中国历史—古
代史—纪传体—英文②《史记》—研究—英文 Ⅳ.①K204.2

中国版本图书馆CIP数据核字(2016)第023123号

名家讲《史记》

编　　者：《文史知识》编辑部
翻　　译：王丽 李莉
出 版 人：荆孝敏
责任编辑：王峰
装帧设计：壹东设计
出版发行：五洲传播出版社
地　　址：北京市海淀区北三环中路31号生产力大楼B座6层
邮　　编：100088
发行电话：010-82005927，010-82007837
网　　址：http://www.cicc.org.cn, http://www.thatsbooks.com
印　　刷：北京利丰雅高长城印刷有限公司
版　　次：2017年1月第1版第1次印刷
开　　本：155×230毫米 1/16
印　　张：12.5
字　　数：200千
定　　价：129.00元